# Mastering Amazon DynamoDB: From Basics to Scalability

Kameron Hussain and Frahaan Hussain

Published by Sonar Publishing, 2024.

MASTERING AMAZON DYNAMODB: FROM BASICS TO SCALABILITY

**First edition. January 30, 2024.**



ISBN: 979-8224275625

Written by Kameron Hussain and Frahaan Hussain.

# Table of Contents

1. Use On-Demand Capacity Mode Wisely
2. Implement Data Retention Policies
3. Use Sparse Indexes
4. Monitor and Adjust Provisioned Throughput
5. Optimize Query and Scan Operations
6. Leverage Reserved Capacity
7. Clean Up Unused Resources
8. Cost Allocation and Monitoring

Section 13.4: Planning for Scalability and Growth

1. Choose the Right Partition Key
2. Monitor and Auto-Scaling
3. Use On-Demand Capacity Mode
4. Implement Caching
5. Data Archiving and Cleanup
6. Leverage Global Tables
7. Disaster Recovery Planning
8. Capacity Planning

Section 13.5: Tips for Efficient Data Retrieval

1. Use Query Instead of Scan
2. Utilize Indexes

6. Enhanced Security Features

7. Data Lake Integration

8. Support for More Data Types

9. Real-time Analytics and Dashboards

10. Developer-Friendly Tools

Section 15.3: The Role of AI and Machine Learning

1. Predictive Analytics

2. Personalization

3. Fraud Detection and Security

4. Natural Language Processing (NLP)

5. Recommendations and Content Generation

6. Operational Efficiency

7. Automated Maintenance

8. Data Anomaly Detection

9. Cost Optimization

10. Continuous Improvement

Section 15.4: DynamoDB in the Context of Big Data

1. Scalability for Big Data

2. Integration with AWS Analytics Services

3. DynamoDB Streams for Real-time Processing

1. Understanding Application Requirements
2. Table Design
3. Efficient Indexing
4. Auto Scaling
5. Caching with DAX
6. Batch Operations
7. Data Consistency
8. Connection Management
9. Handling Large Items
10. Monitoring and Logging
11. Security
12. Global Tables for Multi-Region Applications
13. Time to Live (TTL) for Data Management
14. Utilizing Streams
15. Continuous Backup and Point-in-Time Recovery
16. Query Pagination
17. DynamoDB Local for Development
18. Optimizing Costs

Section 18.2: Managing User Sessions and State

1. Designing Session Management

6. Background Data Sync

7. Conflict Resolution Techniques

8. User Experience during Offline Mode

9. Testing Offline Scenarios

10. Data Compression

11. Security Considerations

12. Managing Local Storage Limits

13. Notifications and Background Tasks

14. Offline Analytics

15. Progressive Web Apps (PWAs)

16. Data Partitioning

17. Handling Large Data Sets

Section 18.5: Case Studies: Successful Mobile and Web Apps

1. E-commerce Platform

2. Social Media App

3. Online Gaming Platform

4. IoT Device Management

5. Content Management System

6. Mobile Health Application

7. Travel Booking Website

15. Backup and Recovery

16. Monitoring and Logging

17. Scalability

Section 19.3: Machine Learning Applications

1. Data Collection and Storage

2. Preparing Data for Machine Learning

3. Integration with Amazon S3

4. Using AWS Glue for ETL

5. Machine Learning with Amazon SageMaker

6. Real-time Predictions

7. Batch Processing with AWS Batch

8. Machine Learning Model Monitoring

9. Feedback Loop for Model Improvement

10. Using DynamoDB as a Feature Store

11. Data Versioning

12. Handling Unstructured Data

13. Security and Compliance

14. Scalable Architecture

15. Cost Optimization

16. Utilizing AWS Marketplace for Algorithms

1. Enhanced Global Tables: DynamoDB Global Tables provide multi-region, highly available solutions. In the future, we can expect enhancements to make global tables even more versatile and easier to manage. This might include simplified setup and configuration, improved conflict resolution mechanisms, and better latency optimizations.

2. Advanced Consistency Models: While DynamoDB offers strong eventual consistency and transactional support, future updates may introduce more advanced consistency models to cater to specific use cases. This could include options for tunable consistency, allowing developers to choose between strong and eventual consistency on a per-operation basis.

3. Advanced Query and Analytics: DynamoDB's query capabilities are already powerful, but AWS might further enhance its querying and analytical capabilities. Expect improvements in query performance, support for more complex analytical queries, and deeper integration with AWS analytics services.

4. Enhanced Security Features: Security is a top priority for AWS, and DynamoDB is no exception. We can anticipate the addition of more fine-grained access control options, enhanced encryption features, and improved auditing and monitoring capabilities.

5. Integration with AI and ML Services: As AI and machine learning become integral to various applications, DynamoDB is likely to offer tighter integration with AWS AI/ML services. This could simplify the process of

using machine learning models for tasks such as predictive analytics and recommendation systems.

6. Serverless Architectures: DynamoDB is already a popular choice for serverless applications. In the future, AWS might provide even more seamless integration with AWS Lambda and other serverless computing services, making it easier to build event-driven applications.

7. Data Lake Integration: With the growing popularity of data lakes for storing and analyzing massive datasets, DynamoDB might offer improved integration with AWS data lake services like Amazon S3 and AWS Glue. This would facilitate easier data movement and analytics.

8. Performance Optimization: AWS continuously works on improving performance. Expect future updates to include optimizations for specific workloads and use cases, ensuring DynamoDB remains a high-performance database service.

9. Developer Tooling: AWS is likely to invest in improving developer tooling around DynamoDB. This could involve enhancements to the AWS SDKs, improved debugging and monitoring tools, and better local development environments.

10. Cost Optimization: While DynamoDB offers cost-effective scaling options, AWS may introduce further cost optimization features, helping businesses save on their DynamoDB expenses without compromising performance.

Section 20.3: The Role of AI and Machine Learning

1. Predictive Analytics: One of the key applications of AI and ML is predictive analytics. DynamoDB can benefit from predictive modeling to forecast future data trends and help businesses make proactive decisions. For example, an e-commerce platform using DynamoDB can employ ML algorithms to predict customer preferences and optimize product recommendations in real-time.

2. Recommendation Engines: AI-powered recommendation engines are crucial for platforms like streaming services, e-commerce, and content websites. DynamoDB can integrate with ML models to provide personalized recommendations based on user behavior and preferences. This enhances user engagement and drives revenue growth.

3. Data Quality and Anomaly Detection: ML algorithms can be employed to detect data anomalies and ensure data quality in DynamoDB. This is especially important for industries like finance, healthcare, and manufacturing, where data accuracy is critical for decision-making and compliance.

4. Natural Language Processing (NLP): DynamoDB can leverage NLP models to extract insights from unstructured text data stored within the database. This enables sentiment analysis, chatbots, and content recommendation systems to provide more intelligent and context-aware responses.

5. Real-time Insights: By integrating DynamoDB with ML services like Amazon SageMaker, businesses can gain real-time insights from their data. ML models can process

streaming data from DynamoDB Streams to identify patterns, detect anomalies, and trigger automated actions.

6. Auto-Scaling with AI: AI-driven auto-scaling can optimize DynamoDB's resource allocation. ML algorithms can predict traffic patterns and adjust read/ write capacity automatically, ensuring optimal performance while minimizing costs.

7. Data Classification and Tagging: ML models can classify and tag data within DynamoDB based on content, sensitivity, or relevance. This aids in data governance, compliance, and access control, making it easier to manage and secure sensitive data.

8. Personalized User Experiences: DynamoDB can store user profiles and behavioral data, allowing businesses to create highly personalized user experiences. ML models can analyze this data to tailor content, offers, and interactions in real-time.

9. Operational Efficiency: AI-driven automation can improve operational efficiency in database management. Tasks like database optimization, indexing, and backup scheduling can be automated, reducing the administrative burden on IT teams.

10. Integration with AI Services: AWS offers a wide range of AI and ML services that can seamlessly integrate with DynamoDB. These include services for training custom ML models, natural language understanding, image recognition, and more.

Section 20.4: DynamoDB in the Context of Big Data

1. Scalability and Performance: DynamoDB's ability to scale horizontally makes it well-suited for big data workloads. It can handle massive amounts of data and provide low-latency responses, ensuring that applications can seamlessly scale to accommodate high data ingestion rates.

2. Data Ingestion: DynamoDB can serve as a landing zone for real-time data ingestion from various sources, such as IoT devices, web applications, and logs. Its fast write capabilities make it suitable for handling streaming data, which is a common requirement in big data processing.

3. Data Storage: While DynamoDB excels in real-time data access, it can also serve as a persistent data store for historical data in big data architectures. By integrating with data lakes and data warehouses, DynamoDB can be part of a comprehensive data storage strategy.

4. Integration with Analytics Services: DynamoDB seamlessly integrates with AWS analytics services like Amazon Redshift, Amazon Athena, and Amazon QuickSight. This allows businesses to run complex queries, analyze historical data, and generate insights from DynamoDB data.

5. Time-Series Data: Many big data use cases involve time-series data, such as sensor readings, logs, and financial market data. DynamoDB's support for TTL (Time to Live) and efficient range queries makes it suitable for storing and querying time-series data.

6. Real-Time Analytics: DynamoDB Streams enables real-time analytics by capturing and processing changes to data in near-real-time. This feature is valuable for applications that require real-time insights and actions based on data updates.

7. Serverless Processing: AWS Lambda, a serverless compute service, can be integrated with DynamoDB to perform data processing and transformation tasks. This serverless approach is cost-effective and scalable, making it ideal for big data workloads.

8. Machine Learning Integration: DynamoDB can store data that is used for training machine learning models. By integrating with AWS SageMaker or other ML services, businesses can leverage DynamoDB data to build predictive models and make data-driven decisions.

9. Data Governance: DynamoDB's security and access control features are crucial for maintaining data governance in big data scenarios. Fine-grained IAM (Identity and Access Management) permissions ensure that only authorized users can access sensitive data.

10. Cost Optimization: DynamoDB offers flexible pricing options, including on-demand and provisioned capacity modes. This flexibility allows organizations to optimize costs based on the specific requirements of their big data workloads.

Section 20.5: Preparing for Future Challenges and Opportunities

1. Stay Informed: Keep abreast of the latest developments in DynamoDB and the broader AWS ecosystem. AWS regularly introduces new features and services, so staying informed is crucial to leverage advancements effectively.

2. Architect for Flexibility: Design your DynamoDB tables and data models with flexibility in mind. Anticipate potential changes in data requirements and usage patterns. Use adaptive schema design principles to accommodate evolving needs.

3. Continuous Optimization: Regularly review and optimize your DynamoDB tables for cost and performance. Utilize tools like AWS Trusted Advisor and Amazon CloudWatch to monitor usage and identify areas for improvement.

4. Security and Compliance: Stay vigilant about security and compliance requirements. DynamoDB provides encryption, access controls, and auditing features to help meet regulatory standards. Regularly audit and update your security policies.

5. Scaling Strategy: As your application scales, revisit your scaling strategy. Evaluate whether to switch between on-demand and provisioned capacity modes based on cost and performance considerations.

6. Disaster Recovery: Ensure that you have robust disaster recovery plans in place. DynamoDB's backup and restore capabilities can be essential in recovering data in case of unexpected outages or data loss.

7. Machine Learning Integration: Explore opportunities to integrate machine learning into your DynamoDB-powered applications. ML can uncover insights from data and automate decision-making processes.

8. Multi-Region Deployment: Consider deploying DynamoDB tables across multiple AWS regions to enhance fault tolerance and reduce latency for global users. Implement global tables for seamless data replication.

9. Monitoring and Alerting: Implement comprehensive monitoring and alerting solutions to detect and respond to issues proactively. AWS CloudWatch and AWS Lambda can automate remediation tasks.

10. Cost Management: Continuously optimize your DynamoDB costs. Leverage cost analysis tools and regularly review your capacity provisioning to avoid overprovisioning.

11. Training and Skill Development: Invest in training and skill development for your team. AWS offers certifications and training courses that can enhance your team's expertise in DynamoDB and related technologies.

12. Community Engagement: Engage with the DynamoDB and AWS community. Participate in forums, attend conferences, and join user groups to learn from others' experiences and share your knowledge.

13. Experiment and Innovate: Encourage a culture of experimentation and innovation. DynamoDB's flexible

schema and serverless capabilities make it an ideal platform for prototyping and exploring new ideas.

14. Documentation and Documentation: Maintain detailed documentation of your DynamoDB tables, schemas, and application architecture. This documentation is invaluable for onboarding new team members and troubleshooting.

15. Feedback Loop: Establish a feedback loop with AWS support and your AWS account team. Provide feedback on your experiences with DynamoDB and share insights on potential improvements.

# Chapter 1: Introduction to Amazon DynamoDB

## 1.1 Understanding NoSQL and DynamoDB

Amazon DynamoDB is a fully managed NoSQL database service offered by Amazon Web Services (AWS). In this section, we will explore the fundamental concepts of NoSQL databases and gain an understanding of how DynamoDB fits into this landscape.

### What is NoSQL?

NoSQL, which stands for "Not Only SQL," is a category of databases designed to store and manage vast amounts of data, often unstructured or semi-structured, in a flexible and scalable manner. NoSQL databases are particularly well-suited for use cases where traditional relational databases may struggle due to their rigid schema and limited scalability.

*Key Characteristics of NoSQL Databases:*

1. **Schemaless**: NoSQL databases do not enforce a fixed schema, allowing you to store data with varying structures without the need for predefined tables or columns.
2. **Horizontal Scalability**: Many NoSQL databases are designed to scale horizontally, distributing data across multiple servers or nodes to handle high volumes of traffic and large datasets.
3. **High Performance**: NoSQL databases are optimized for read and write operations, making them suitable for applications requiring low-latency data access.
4. **Flexibility**: These databases support various data models,

including document-oriented, key-value, column-family, and graph databases, making them adaptable to different use cases.

## Why Choose NoSQL?

NoSQL databases offer several advantages that make them attractive for modern application development:

- **Flexible Data Models**: NoSQL databases can accommodate changing data structures, making them ideal for agile development and evolving data requirements.

- **Scalability**: With the ability to scale horizontally, NoSQL databases can handle growing workloads by adding more nodes to the cluster.

- **High Availability**: Many NoSQL databases are built with redundancy and failover mechanisms, ensuring data remains accessible even in the event of hardware failures.

- **Performance**: They are optimized for high-speed data access, making them suitable for real-time applications and big data analytics.

## Introduction to Amazon DynamoDB

Amazon DynamoDB is a fully managed NoSQL database service that offers seamless scalability, low-latency data access, and high availability. It is designed to handle applications with demanding read and write requirements while simplifying database administration.

DynamoDB is based on a key-value data model, where data is organized into tables, and each item in a table is uniquely identified by a primary key. This design provides fast and predictable performance, making it an excellent choice for use cases such as e-commerce, gaming, IoT, and more.

***Key Features of Amazon DynamoDB:***

- **Managed Service**: AWS takes care of the operational aspects of DynamoDB, including hardware provisioning, data replication, and software patching, allowing you to focus on building applications.

- **Scalability**: DynamoDB can automatically scale to handle varying workloads and traffic patterns, eliminating the need for manual capacity planning.

- **Multi-Region Replication**: You can replicate your data across multiple AWS regions to ensure high availability and disaster recovery.

- **Security**: DynamoDB offers robust security features, including data encryption at rest and in transit, fine-grained access control through IAM roles, and integration with AWS Identity and Access Management (IAM).

- **Serverless Options**: With DynamoDB, you can build serverless applications using AWS Lambda and other services, enabling you to pay only for the resources you consume.

- **Global Secondary Indexes (GSI)**: GSIs allow you to efficiently query your data by attributes other than the primary key, providing flexibility in querying and data retrieval.

In the following sections of this chapter, we will delve deeper into the evolution of DynamoDB, its key benefits, and how it compares to traditional databases. We will also explore various use cases and industry applications that leverage the power of DynamoDB to meet their data storage and retrieval needs.

Stay tuned to gain a comprehensive understanding of Amazon DynamoDB and how it can revolutionize your data management strategies.

---

## 1.2 The Evolution of Amazon DynamoDB

Amazon DynamoDB has undergone significant evolution since its inception, and it continues to adapt to meet the evolving needs of modern applications. In this section, we'll explore the key milestones and changes in the history of DynamoDB.

### Early Origins

DynamoDB's roots can be traced back to Amazon's internal infrastructure needs. Amazon required a highly scalable, distributed, and fault-tolerant database system to support its e-commerce platform. To address these requirements, Amazon engineers developed Dynamo, an internal NoSQL database system.

### DynamoDB's Public Debut

In 2012, Amazon introduced DynamoDB to the public as a fully managed NoSQL database service on AWS. This marked the beginning of DynamoDB's journey as a widely available and widely adopted cloud database solution. Its key features, such as automatic scaling, managed infrastructure, and seamless replication, quickly attracted developers and businesses.

## Introduction of Streams

One of the significant additions to DynamoDB was the introduction of DynamoDB Streams. This feature, released in 2014, allowed developers to capture changes to data in real-time. DynamoDB Streams opened the door for building applications that required event-driven architectures, real-time analytics, and auditing capabilities.

```
# Example of reading data from a DynamoDB Stream in Python using AWS SDK

import boto3

# Initialize the DynamoDB client

dynamodb = boto3.client('dynamodb')

# Specify the stream ARN

stream_arn = 'arn:aws:dynamodb:us-east-1:123456789012:table/MyTable/stream/2022-01-01T00:00:00.000'

# Create a DynamoDB Streams client

streams = boto3.client('dynamodbstreams')

# Get the latest stream shard iterator

response = streams.get_shard_iterator(

StreamArn=stream_arn,
```

```
ShardId='000000000000'
)
# Retrieve records from the stream
shard_iterator = response['ShardIterator']
records = streams.get_records(ShardIterator=shard_iterator)
for record in records['Records']:
print(record)
```

## Global Tables

In 2017, Amazon DynamoDB introduced Global Tables, a feature that enables automatic and seamless replication of data across multiple AWS regions. This was a game-changer for applications requiring high availability and disaster recovery. Global Tables expanded DynamoDB's reach to a global scale.

## On-Demand Billing Mode

DynamoDB introduced the On-Demand billing mode in 2018, allowing users to pay for the resources they consume without the need for capacity planning or provisioning. This flexible pricing model made DynamoDB more accessible to startups and applications with unpredictable workloads.

## Adaptive Capacity

To enhance cost-effectiveness and performance predictability, DynamoDB introduced Adaptive Capacity in 2019. This feature allows tables to automatically manage their read and write capacities, optimizing resource utilization and reducing costs.

### Continuous Innovation

Amazon DynamoDB continues to evolve with regular updates, introducing features like PartiQL support, strong consistency for global secondary indexes (GSI), and more. It remains a cornerstone of the AWS data ecosystem, serving a wide range of use cases across industries.

In the upcoming sections of this book, we will dive deeper into DynamoDB's features, use cases, and best practices, enabling you to harness the power of this dynamic database service for your own applications. Stay tuned for a comprehensive exploration of Amazon DynamoDB.

---

## 1.3 Key Features and Benefits

Amazon DynamoDB offers a rich set of features and benefits that make it a popular choice for building scalable and high-performance applications. In this section, we'll explore the key features and advantages of DynamoDB that set it apart from other database solutions.

### 1.3.1 Fully Managed Service

DynamoDB is a fully managed NoSQL database service provided by AWS. This means that AWS takes care of the underlying infrastructure, including server provisioning, data replication, and maintenance tasks. As a developer, you can focus solely on building and optimizing your application, without the burden of managing the database infrastructure.

### 1.3.2 Seamless Scalability

One of the standout features of DynamoDB is its ability to scale seamlessly to accommodate varying workloads. Whether your application experiences sudden traffic spikes or steady growth, DynamoDB can automatically adjust its capacity to handle the load. This eliminates the need for manual capacity planning and ensures that your application remains responsive under all conditions.

```
# Example of increasing read capacity for a DynamoDB table using AWS SDK

import boto3

# Initialize the DynamoDB client

dynamodb = boto3.client('dynamodb')

# Specify the table name

table_name = 'MyTable'

# Increase read capacity units

dynamodb.update_table(

TableName=table_name,

ProvisionedThroughput={

'ReadCapacityUnits': 2000 # New read capacity units

}

)
```

### 1.3.3 Low-Latency Data Access

DynamoDB is designed for high-performance data access. It offers single-digit millisecond latency for read and write operations, making it suitable for real-time applications that require rapid data retrieval. This low-latency access ensures that your users receive a responsive experience, even when dealing with large datasets.

### 1.3.4 High Availability and Durability

Amazon DynamoDB provides high availability by replicating data across multiple Availability Zones within a region. This redundancy ensures that your data remains accessible even in the event of hardware failures or other disruptions. Additionally, DynamoDB offers data backup and restore capabilities, further enhancing data durability.

### 1.3.5 Security Features

Security is a top priority for DynamoDB. It offers several security features, including:

- **Data Encryption**: DynamoDB supports encryption at rest, ensuring that your data is protected on disk.

- **Data Encryption in Transit**: All data transferred to and from DynamoDB is encrypted using industry-standard protocols.

- **Access Control**: You can define fine-grained access control policies using AWS Identity and Access Management (IAM) roles to restrict who can access your DynamoDB resources.

### 1.3.6 Global Tables for Multi-Region Replication

Global Tables, introduced in DynamoDB, allow you to replicate your data across multiple AWS regions. This feature enhances availability and disaster recovery capabilities by providing a global presence for your application. It ensures that users in different regions can access your data with low-latency and high reliability.

### 1.3.7 Flexible Data Models

DynamoDB offers flexibility in data modeling. While it is a key-value store at its core, you can use composite primary keys and secondary indexes to query data in various ways. This adaptability makes DynamoDB suitable for a wide range of use cases, from simple key-value storage to complex querying scenarios.

### 1.3.8 Pay-Per-Usage Pricing

DynamoDB offers a flexible pricing model that allows you to pay only for the resources you consume. With On-Demand and Provisioned capacity modes, you can choose the pricing model that best aligns with your application's needs. This cost-effectiveness is particularly advantageous for startups and applications with unpredictable workloads.

In the upcoming chapters of this book, we will delve deeper into each of these features and explore practical examples and best practices for utilizing DynamoDB effectively. By understanding these features and benefits, you'll be well-equipped to harness the power of Amazon DynamoDB for your own projects and applications.

# 1.4 Comparing DynamoDB with Traditional Databases

When choosing a database solution for your application, it's essential to consider how Amazon DynamoDB compares to traditional relational databases. In this section, we'll examine the key differences between DynamoDB and traditional databases, highlighting the advantages and trade-offs of each approach.

## Data Model

*DynamoDB:*

- DynamoDB is a NoSQL database that uses a key-value data model.
- Data in DynamoDB is organized into tables, and each item within a table is uniquely identified by a primary key.
- DynamoDB allows flexible schemaless data storage, where different items within the same table can have different attributes.

*Traditional Databases:*

- Traditional relational databases use a structured schema with tables, rows, and columns.
- Data in relational databases must conform to the predefined schema, which can be inflexible for evolving data requirements.

## Scalability

*DynamoDB:*

- DynamoDB is designed for seamless horizontal scalability.
- It can automatically handle increased workloads by adding more capacity units, making it suitable for applications with unpredictable traffic patterns.

*Traditional Databases:*

- Scaling traditional databases can be complex and often requires manual intervention.
- Scaling vertically (adding more resources to a single server) has limitations and can be costly.

## Performance

*DynamoDB:*

- DynamoDB offers low-latency read and write operations, typically in the single-digit millisecond range.
- Its performance is consistent even as the data volume grows, thanks to automatic partitioning.

*Traditional Databases:*

- Performance in traditional databases can degrade as the dataset size increases, necessitating careful optimization and indexing.

## Schema Evolution

*DynamoDB:*

- DynamoDB allows you to add and remove attributes from items without altering the entire table schema.

- This flexibility makes it well-suited for agile development and accommodating changing data structures.

*Traditional Databases:*

- Traditional databases require schema changes and migrations when altering data structures, which can be a complex and time-consuming process.

## Querying

*DynamoDB:*

- DynamoDB provides efficient querying capabilities based on primary keys and secondary indexes.

- It excels at key-based lookups and range queries.

***Traditional Databases:***

- Traditional databases offer powerful querying capabilities, including complex SQL queries that can join multiple tables.

- Query optimization and indexing are critical for query performance.

## ACID Transactions

***DynamoDB:***

- DynamoDB supports transactions within a single item or across multiple items in the same table.

- It provides strong consistency for read operations.

***Traditional Databases:***

- Traditional databases follow the ACID (Atomicity, Consistency, Isolation, Durability) properties and offer robust transaction support.

## Cost

***DynamoDB:***

- DynamoDB offers pay-per-usage pricing, allowing you to pay for the resources you consume.

- On-Demand and Provisioned capacity modes offer flexibility in cost management.

*Traditional Databases:*

- Traditional databases often involve upfront licensing and hardware costs, as well as ongoing maintenance expenses.

## Use Cases

*DynamoDB:*

- DynamoDB is well-suited for use cases with high scalability and low-latency requirements, such as e-commerce platforms, gaming, and IoT applications.
- It shines in scenarios where data volumes can vary significantly.

*Traditional Databases:*

- Traditional databases are commonly used for applications with structured data and complex queries, such as financial systems and reporting.

## Conclusion

While both Amazon DynamoDB and traditional relational databases have their strengths and use cases, DynamoDB stands out as a versatile and scalable solution for modern, high-performance applications. By understanding the differences outlined above, you can make an informed decision when selecting the right database technology for your specific project requirements.

## 1.5 Use Cases and Industry Applications

Amazon DynamoDB's versatility and scalability make it suitable for a wide range of use cases across various industries. In this section, we will explore some of the common use cases and industry applications where DynamoDB excels.

### 1.5.1 E-Commerce Platforms

E-commerce platforms require a database that can handle high volumes of product data, user profiles, and transaction records while delivering low-latency responses. DynamoDB is an excellent choice for e-commerce applications because of its seamless scalability, fast data access, and high availability. It allows online retailers to manage product catalogs, track inventory, process orders, and provide personalized user experiences efficiently.

### 1.5.2 Gaming

Online gaming applications often deal with dynamic and real-time data, such as player profiles, game states, leaderboards, and in-game transactions. DynamoDB's ability to handle unpredictable traffic spikes and deliver low-latency responses makes it a preferred choice for gaming backends. Game developers can use DynamoDB to create responsive and highly available gaming experiences, even during peak usage periods.

### 1.5.3 Internet of Things (IoT)

IoT devices generate massive volumes of data, from sensor readings to device telemetry. DynamoDB's ability to handle high write throughput and real-time data ingestion is invaluable for IoT applications. It can store and process data from sensors, monitor device states, and trigger actions based on incoming data.

DynamoDB's global tables feature ensures that data is accessible from various geographic locations, supporting global IoT deployments.

### 1.5.4 Content Management Systems (CMS)

Content management systems, whether for websites, blogs, or digital media, require a reliable and scalable database to store content, user profiles, and access logs. DynamoDB's low-latency data access and serverless options make it a suitable choice for CMS applications. Developers can build responsive and cost-effective content management systems that scale with traffic and content growth.

### 1.5.5 Financial Services

In the financial services industry, data security, high availability, and low-latency access are paramount. DynamoDB's strong consistency, data encryption features, and multi-region replication make it a compelling choice for applications such as transaction processing, fraud detection, and customer account management. It ensures that sensitive financial data is protected and accessible to users globally.

### 1.5.6 Healthcare and Life Sciences

Healthcare and life sciences applications deal with critical patient data, medical records, and research findings. DynamoDB's compliance with industry regulations, such as HIPAA, combined with its scalability and durability, makes it suitable for storing and managing healthcare data. Researchers and healthcare providers can leverage DynamoDB for real-time data analysis and secure data storage.

### 1.5.7 Ad Tech and Marketing

Advertising technology (ad tech) platforms require databases that can handle ad impressions, user profiles, and campaign analytics. DynamoDB's ability to process large volumes of data with low-latency access is beneficial for ad tech applications. Marketers can use DynamoDB to track user behavior, personalize ad targeting, and optimize ad campaigns in real-time.

### 1.5.8 Logistics and Supply Chain

Logistics and supply chain management involve tracking inventory, shipments, and order fulfillment. DynamoDB's scalability and real-time data processing capabilities support logistics applications that require rapid updates and access to inventory status. It helps businesses streamline operations, reduce errors, and enhance supply chain visibility.

### 1.5.9 Online Marketplaces

Online marketplaces connect buyers and sellers, managing vast amounts of product listings, user accounts, and transaction history. DynamoDB's scalability and performance ensure that online marketplaces can handle a growing number of listings and users. It supports features like search and recommendation engines to enhance the user experience.

### 1.5.10 Social Media and User Engagement

Social media platforms and user engagement applications rely on databases to store user-generated content, activity feeds, and user profiles. DynamoDB's ability to handle high write and read workloads enables real-time updates and content delivery. It helps create interactive and engaging social media experiences.

These are just a few examples of the diverse use cases and industry applications where Amazon DynamoDB shines. Its flexibility, scalability, and low-latency data access make it a valuable tool for developers and businesses looking to build high-performance, cloud-native applications across various domains. In the subsequent chapters, we will delve deeper into each use case, providing guidance and best practices for leveraging DynamoDB effectively in specific scenarios.

# Chapter 2: Setting Up with Amazon DynamoDB

## 2.1 Creating an AWS Account

To begin working with Amazon DynamoDB, you'll need an AWS (Amazon Web Services) account. AWS provides a free tier with limited usage to get started, and it offers various pricing plans based on your needs. In this section, we'll guide you through the process of creating an AWS account.

### Steps to Create an AWS Account

1. **Visit the AWS Website**: Open your web browser and navigate to the AWS website at https://aws.amazon.com/.
2. **Click on "Create an AWS Account"**: You'll find this option at the top right corner of the AWS homepage. Click on it to start the registration process.
3. **Provide Your Email Address**: Enter your email address, and then click the "Next" button.
4. **Password and Account Information**: Create a password for your AWS account. You'll also need to provide some basic information, including your name, company name (if applicable), and contact information.
5. **Contact Information**: Enter your contact information, including your phone number and address. This information is used for account verification and billing purposes.
6. **Payment Information**: You'll need to provide your payment details to verify your identity. AWS may charge a small, refundable amount to your card for verification purposes.

7. **Choose a Support Plan**: AWS offers a range of support plans, including a free basic plan. Choose the plan that suits your needs or opt for the free plan.
8. **Review and Confirm**: Review the information you've provided and read the AWS Customer Agreement and the AWS Service Terms. Once you're satisfied, click the "Create Account and Continue" button.
9. **Phone Verification**: AWS may require phone verification for added security. Enter the code sent to your phone to verify your identity.
10. **Account Setup**: After successful verification, you can proceed with setting up your AWS account. This includes creating an AWS Identity and Access Management (IAM) user, which is crucial for managing access to AWS services securely.
11. **Access AWS Management Console**: Once your account is set up, you can access the AWS Management Console, where you can manage your AWS resources, including DynamoDB.

## AWS Free Tier

As a new AWS user, you are eligible for the AWS Free Tier, which provides limited free usage of AWS services, including DynamoDB, for 12 months. This allows you to explore and experiment with DynamoDB without incurring charges during the free tier period.

Keep in mind that while the AWS Free Tier offers cost-free usage for eligible services within certain usage limits, it's essential to monitor your usage to avoid unexpected charges outside of the free tier limits.

By following the steps outlined in this section, you can create an AWS account and access the AWS Management Console, where you'll be ready to start setting up and using Amazon DynamoDB for your database needs.

## 2.2 Navigating the AWS Management Console

Once you have successfully created your AWS account, you can start navigating the AWS Management Console, the web-based interface for managing your AWS resources, including Amazon DynamoDB. In this section, we'll introduce you to the AWS Management Console and provide an overview of its key components.

### Logging into the AWS Management Console

To access the AWS Management Console, follow these steps:

1. Open your web browser and go to https://aws.amazon.com/.
2. Click on "Sign In to the Console" at the top right corner of the AWS homepage.
3. Enter the email address and password associated with your AWS account.
4. Click the "Sign In" button to log in.

### AWS Management Console Overview

The AWS Management Console provides a user-friendly interface for managing AWS services and resources. Here's an overview of its main components:

*1. Services Menu:*

- Located at the top left corner of the console, the Services menu allows you to navigate to different AWS services, including DynamoDB. You can search for services by name or category.

*2. Dashboard:*

- The Dashboard provides an overview of your AWS resources, including service health, recent resource changes, and cost-related information.

*3. Navigation Pane:*

- The Navigation Pane, on the left side of the console, displays a list of AWS services and categories. You can expand categories to access specific services.

*4. Resource Groups:*

- Resource Groups allow you to organize AWS resources across services into logical groups for easier management.

*5. AWS Global Region:*

- AWS is divided into regions, each consisting of multiple Availability Zones. You can choose the region where you want to create and manage your resources.

*6. Console Search Bar:*

• The search bar at the top of the console allows you to quickly search for AWS services, resources, and documentation.

*7. Support and Notifications:*

• You can access AWS Support, view notifications, and access documentation and resources from the top right corner of the console.

*8. User Menu:*

• The user menu displays your account name and provides options for managing your account, setting preferences, and signing out.

## Navigating to Amazon DynamoDB

To navigate to Amazon DynamoDB in the AWS Management Console:

1. Sign in to the AWS Management Console as described earlier.
2. Click on the "Services" menu at the top left corner of the console.
3. In the "Database" section, you can find "DynamoDB." You can either click on it directly or use the search bar to find and select DynamoDB.

Once you access the DynamoDB service in the console, you can start creating and managing your DynamoDB tables, configuring settings, and performing various database operations.

In the upcoming chapters, we'll delve deeper into using DynamoDB through the AWS Management Console and other AWS tools and SDKs, allowing you to effectively work with this NoSQL database service.

---

## 2.3 Setting Up DynamoDB

Setting up Amazon DynamoDB involves configuring essential settings, permissions, and access controls to ensure your database operates securely and efficiently. In this section, we'll guide you through the initial setup steps for DynamoDB.

### 2.3.1 Access Control with AWS Identity and Access Management (IAM)

IAM (Identity and Access Management) is a critical component of AWS security. It allows you to control access to your AWS resources, including DynamoDB. Here are some key IAM considerations when setting up DynamoDB:

- **User Permissions**: Assign IAM user roles and permissions to individuals or applications that need access to DynamoDB. Follow the principle of least privilege to grant only the necessary permissions.

- **Resource Policies**: DynamoDB also supports resource-based policies, allowing you to control access to specific tables or resources. You can define policies that specify who can perform actions on DynamoDB resources.

- **Authentication**: Use IAM roles and temporary security credentials to enable applications to securely access DynamoDB without exposing long-term AWS access keys.

## 2.3.2 Table Creation and Configuration

To start using DynamoDB effectively, you need to create tables and configure them according to your data modeling requirements. Here are the steps for creating a DynamoDB table:

1. **Log in to the AWS Management Console.**
2. **Navigate to DynamoDB** by selecting it from the Services menu or using the search bar.
3. **Click "Create Table"** to begin the table creation process.
4. **Specify the table name** and the primary key, which consists of one or two attributes. The primary key uniquely identifies each item in the table.
5. **Choose the provisioned throughput** capacity mode (or On-Demand if you prefer pay-as-you-go pricing). Provisioned throughput involves specifying read and write capacity units, while On-Demand automatically adjusts capacity based on usage.
6. **Configure additional settings** such as auto scaling, encryption, and stream settings as needed for your application.
7. **Click "Create"** to create the table.

Once the table is created, you can start inserting data, defining secondary indexes, and performing various operations on it.

### 2.3.3 Data Ingestion and Management

DynamoDB supports various methods for ingesting data into your tables, including manual data entry, batch loading, and real-time data ingestion using DynamoDB Streams. You can use the AWS SDKs or command-line tools to interact with your DynamoDB tables programmatically.

Here's a brief example of inserting data into a DynamoDB table using the AWS SDK for Python (Boto3):

```
import boto3

# Initialize DynamoDB client

dynamodb = boto3.client('dynamodb')

# Define the table name

table_name = 'MyTable'

# Define the item to insert

item = {

'PrimaryKey': {'S': '12345'},

'AttributeName': {'N': '42'}

}

# Insert the item into the table

response = dynamodb.put_item(TableName=table_name, Item=item)

# Check the response for success
```

```
if response['ResponseMetadata']['HTTPStatusCode'] == 200:
print('Item inserted successfully.')
```

## 2.3.4 Monitoring and Alerts

Monitoring is crucial to ensure the health and performance of your DynamoDB tables. AWS provides CloudWatch, a monitoring service, to help you track various metrics and set up alarms based on specific conditions.

You can configure CloudWatch alarms to notify you when, for example, provisioned throughput capacity is approaching its limits or when there are issues with your DynamoDB tables. Setting up alarms helps you proactively address potential problems and maintain the reliability of your database.

## 2.3.5 Backup and Restore

DynamoDB offers backup and restore capabilities to protect your data from accidental deletions or data corruption. You can create backups of your tables and set up retention policies to automatically delete old backups. In case of data loss, you can restore your tables to a specific point in time.

By configuring these backup and restore settings, you ensure the long-term durability and availability of your data stored in DynamoDB.

In this section, we've outlined the initial setup steps for Amazon DynamoDB, including access control, table creation, data management, monitoring, and backup and restore. Properly configuring these aspects is essential for a secure and reliable DynamoDB environment. In the upcoming chapters, we'll explore these topics in more detail and provide best practices for optimizing your DynamoDB setup.

## 2.4 Understanding Pricing and Billing

When using Amazon DynamoDB, it's essential to understand its pricing model and billing structure to manage costs effectively. DynamoDB offers various pricing options and factors that can impact your expenses. In this section, we'll explore key pricing considerations for DynamoDB.

### 2.4.1 On-Demand Capacity Mode

DynamoDB offers two capacity modes: On-Demand and Provisioned. In On-Demand capacity mode, you pay for the actual read and write requests your application makes to DynamoDB. There are no upfront costs or ongoing commitments. On-Demand capacity mode is suitable for applications with unpredictable workloads, as it automatically scales capacity to handle traffic spikes.

### 2.4.2 Provisioned Capacity Mode

Provisioned capacity mode allows you to specify the amount of read and write capacity units your DynamoDB table can handle. You pay a fixed hourly rate based on the provisioned capacity, regardless of whether you fully utilize it. Provisioned capacity mode is more cost-effective for steady-state workloads with predictable traffic patterns.

### 2.4.3 Read and Write Capacity Units

In DynamoDB, read and write capacity units are measures of throughput. One read capacity unit allows one strongly consistent read per second or two eventually consistent reads per second for items up to 4 KB in size. One write capacity unit allows one write per second for items up to 1 KB in size. If your items are larger, you'll consume more capacity units.

### 2.4.4 Storage Costs

DynamoDB charges for the storage your tables consume. You pay for the actual data stored, including indexed data. The cost depends on the provisioned storage and the backup retention policy you set up. DynamoDB's automatic data compression can help reduce storage costs.

### 2.4.5 Data Transfer Costs

Data transfer costs may apply when your DynamoDB tables are accessed from different AWS regions or if your application interacts with DynamoDB over the internet. Data transfer between DynamoDB and other AWS services within the same region is usually free.

### 2.4.6 Global Tables

If you use DynamoDB Global Tables for multi-region replication, you'll incur additional data transfer and storage costs associated with replicating data across regions. However, Global Tables provide high availability and disaster recovery benefits.

### 2.4.7 Free Tier and Pricing Calculator

AWS offers a Free Tier for DynamoDB, allowing limited free usage for 12 months. This can be an excellent way to get started and explore DynamoDB without incurring charges. Additionally, AWS provides a Pricing Calculator that allows you to estimate your

DynamoDB costs based on your expected usage and capacity requirements.

### 2.4.8 Cost Optimization Strategies

To optimize DynamoDB costs:

- **Monitor Usage**: Regularly review your AWS billing and usage reports to identify cost drivers and optimize your provisioned capacity.

- **Use Auto Scaling**: In Provisioned capacity mode, enable auto scaling to automatically adjust capacity based on your application's needs, reducing overprovisioning.

- **Leverage On-Demand**: Consider using On-Demand capacity mode for applications with varying workloads to avoid overprovisioning.

- **Efficient Data Modeling**: Design your data model efficiently to minimize the number of reads and writes required.

- **Use TTL (Time to Live)**: Implement TTL to automatically expire and delete data that is no longer needed, reducing storage costs.

- **Reserved Capacity**: If you have predictable workloads, consider purchasing reserved capacity to lower your provisioned capacity costs.

By understanding these pricing considerations and implementing cost optimization strategies, you can effectively manage your

DynamoDB expenses while ensuring your application's performance and reliability.

In the following chapters, we will delve deeper into specific DynamoDB features and best practices to help you make cost-effective decisions when using this powerful NoSQL database service.

---

## 2.5 Security and Access Management

Security is paramount when using Amazon DynamoDB to store and manage your data. AWS provides a robust set of tools and features to help you secure your DynamoDB resources and control access to your data. In this section, we'll explore key security considerations and best practices for DynamoDB.

### 2.5.1 Identity and Access Management (IAM)

IAM (Identity and Access Management) allows you to control who can access your DynamoDB resources and what actions they can perform. Here are some IAM best practices for DynamoDB:

- **Least Privilege**: Follow the principle of least privilege when defining IAM policies. Assign permissions only to the necessary resources and actions.

- **Use IAM Roles**: Instead of embedding access keys in your application code or configuration, use IAM roles to grant temporary permissions to your application. This reduces the risk of exposure.

- **MFA (Multi-Factor Authentication)**: Require MFA for IAM users who have privileged access to your AWS account.

### 2.5.2 VPC (Virtual Private Cloud) Endpoints

To enhance security, you can access DynamoDB through VPC endpoints. VPC endpoints allow you to connect to DynamoDB without exposing your data to the public internet. This provides an additional layer of security for your database access.

### 2.5.3 Encryption

Data encryption is crucial to protect your data at rest and in transit. DynamoDB offers the following encryption options:

- **Encryption at Rest**: DynamoDB encrypts your data at rest by default using AES-256 encryption. You can also use customer-managed keys (CMKs) with AWS Key Management Service (KMS) for added control.

- **Encryption in Transit**: Data sent between your application and DynamoDB is encrypted using SSL/TLS encryption. Ensure your application is configured to use SSL/TLS when communicating with DynamoDB.

### 2.5.4 Fine-Grained Access Control

DynamoDB provides fine-grained access control using features like Identity and Access Management (IAM) policies, resource-based policies, and Amazon Cognito. You can restrict access to specific tables and actions, allowing you to implement security at the table and item level.

### 2.5.5 Auditing and Logging

Enable auditing and logging to monitor and track access to your DynamoDB tables. AWS CloudTrail records API activity, providing an audit trail of actions taken on your DynamoDB resources. You can set up CloudTrail to send logs to Amazon CloudWatch Logs for real-time monitoring and analysis.

### 2.5.6 Data Classification and Tagging

Implement data classification and tagging to label your DynamoDB tables and resources with appropriate security levels. This helps you apply consistent security controls and track data access more effectively.

### 2.5.7 Compliance and Regulations

If your application handles sensitive data, such as healthcare or financial information, ensure that your DynamoDB setup complies with industry-specific regulations, such as HIPAA, GDPR, or PCI DSS. AWS offers resources and services to help you meet these compliance requirements.

### 2.5.8 Backup and Disaster Recovery

Secure your data by implementing backup and disaster recovery strategies. DynamoDB offers backup and restore capabilities, allowing you to recover your data in case of accidental deletion or data corruption. Regularly test your recovery procedures to ensure data availability.

### 2.5.9 Security Best Practices

To enhance DynamoDB security, consider the following best practices:

- Regularly review and update IAM policies to maintain the principle of least privilege.

- Enable VPC endpoints to restrict network access to DynamoDB.

- Monitor and analyze CloudTrail logs for security-related events.

- Implement encryption both at rest and in transit.

- Conduct regular security audits and vulnerability assessments.

- Educate your development and operations teams about security best practices.

By implementing these security considerations and best practices, you can help ensure the confidentiality, integrity, and availability of your data stored in Amazon DynamoDB. Security should be an integral part of your DynamoDB deployment strategy to protect your valuable data assets.

# Chapter 3: DynamoDB Core Concepts

## 3.1 Tables, Items, and Attributes

In Amazon DynamoDB, tables, items, and attributes are fundamental concepts that shape how you organize and store your data. Understanding these core concepts is crucial for designing an efficient and scalable database schema.

### 3.1.1 Tables

Tables in DynamoDB are the top-level containers for your data. Think of a table as a collection of related information. Each table consists of items, and you can have multiple tables in your DynamoDB database. Tables are schema-less, meaning that you can have different attributes for each item within the same table.

When designing your DynamoDB schema, consider the access patterns and query requirements for your application. Tables should be designed based on the type of data they will store and how that data will be accessed.

### 3.1.2 Items

Items are individual records within a DynamoDB table. Each item is uniquely identified by its primary key, which can consist of one or two attributes:

- **Partition Key**: A single attribute that uniquely identifies an item within a table. It determines the physical location where the item is stored in DynamoDB.
- **Sort Key (Optional)**: If specified, the sort key allows you to create a composite primary key. The combination

of the partition key and sort key must be unique within the table.

Items can also have additional attributes, which are essentially key-value pairs that store the actual data. DynamoDB supports various data types for attributes, including strings, numbers, binary data, lists, maps, and more.

### 3.1.3 Attributes

Attributes are the data elements within an item. Each attribute has a name and a value. In DynamoDB, attributes can be of various data types, including:

- **Scalar Types**: These are single-value types such as strings, numbers, and binary data.

- **Document Types**: Document types, such as lists and maps, allow you to store complex data structures within attributes.

- **Set Types**: Set types can store multiple values of the same data type without duplicates. DynamoDB supports string sets, number sets, and binary sets.

When designing your DynamoDB schema, carefully choose the data types for your attributes to ensure efficient data storage and retrieval.

### 3.1.4 Example Schema

To illustrate these concepts, consider an example schema for a DynamoDB table that stores information about books:

- **Table Name**: Books

- **Primary Key:**

  – Partition Key: ISBN (a unique identifier for each book)

  – Sort Key: Title (to allow efficient querying by book title)

- **Attributes:**

  – Author (String)

  – PublicationYear (Number)

  – Genre (String)

  – Ratings (Number Set)

  – Reviews (Map)

In this example, each item in the Books table represents a book, with its ISBN serving as the partition key and its title as the sort key. Additional attributes store information about the author, publication year, genre, ratings, and reviews.

Understanding these core concepts of tables, items, and attributes is essential as you design and interact with DynamoDB databases. In the following sections of this chapter, we will explore primary keys, read and write capacity units, indexes, and best practices for designing efficient DynamoDB schemas.

## 3.2 Primary Keys: Partition and Sort Keys

Primary keys are a fundamental aspect of your DynamoDB schema, defining how data is organized within a table and how it can be efficiently queried. In DynamoDB, a primary key consists of one or two attributes: the partition key and the sort key (optional). Let's explore these primary key components in detail.

### 3.2.1 Partition Key

The partition key is a required attribute that uniquely identifies an item within a DynamoDB table. When you create a table, you must specify a partition key, and DynamoDB uses it to distribute data across multiple physical storage partitions. Each partition key value determines the location where an item is stored.

Choosing the right partition key is critical for evenly distributing data and ensuring efficient read and write operations. Consider the following guidelines when selecting a partition key:

- **Uniqueness**: Partition key values must be unique within the table. This uniqueness constraint allows DynamoDB to quickly locate items.

- **Diversity**: Select a partition key that distributes data evenly. Avoid hot partitions, where a small subset of partition key values receive a disproportionate amount of traffic.

- **Query Patterns**: Consider your application's query patterns. The partition key should align with the primary access patterns of your data.

For example, in a table that stores customer orders, the customer's unique ID might serve as a suitable partition key because it evenly distributes data and aligns with queries that retrieve a specific customer's orders.

### 3.2.2 Sort Key (Composite Primary Key)

The sort key, also known as the range key, is an optional attribute that, when used, creates a composite primary key along with the partition key. The combination of the partition key and sort key values must be unique within the table.

The sort key is valuable for organizing related items together within the same partition. It allows you to perform range queries and efficiently retrieve a subset of items based on their sort key values. Sort keys enable a flexible querying approach, enabling you to retrieve data in ascending or descending order by the sort key.

For example, in a table that stores product reviews, you might use a composite primary key with the product ID as the partition key and the review timestamp as the sort key. This would allow you to efficiently query reviews for a specific product within a given time range.

### 3.2.3 Example of Primary Key

Let's consider an example of a DynamoDB table that stores information about music albums:

- **Table Name**: Albums

- **Primary Key**:

  – Partition Key: Artist (String)

  – Sort Key: AlbumTitle (String)

- **Attributes**:

  – ReleaseYear (Number)

  – Genre (String)

– Rating (Number)

– Tracks (Number)

In this example, the primary key consists of the Artist attribute as the partition key and the AlbumTitle attribute as the sort key. This schema allows for efficient querying of albums by a specific artist and sorting albums by title within each artist's collection.

Understanding the role of primary keys, both partition and sort keys, is crucial when designing your DynamoDB schema. Properly chosen primary keys can significantly impact the performance and efficiency of your database queries. In the subsequent sections, we will delve into secondary indexes, read and write capacity units, and other DynamoDB concepts to help you design and optimize your database schema.

---

## 3.3 Understanding Read and Write Capacity Units

In Amazon DynamoDB, read and write capacity units (RCUs and WCUs) are critical for managing the performance and cost of your database operations. These capacity units determine how much throughput your table can handle and are billed based on your usage. Let's explore RCUs and WCUs in more detail.

### 3.3.1 Read Capacity Units (RCUs)

RCUs represent the provisioned capacity for reading data from your DynamoDB table. Each RCU allows for one strongly consistent read per second for items up to 4 KB in size or two eventually consistent reads per second for the same item size. Strongly consistent reads guarantee that you receive the latest data, while eventually consistent reads may return slightly outdated data but are more cost-effective.

When you provision RCUs for your table, you specify the maximum number of reads per second your table can handle. For example, if you provision 100 RCUs, your table can handle up to 100 strongly consistent reads per second or up to 200 eventually consistent reads per second for items up to 4 KB.

To optimize your RCU provisioning, consider the following factors:

- **Access Patterns**: Analyze your application's read patterns. Provision RCUs based on the number of read operations your application performs per second.

- **Item Size**: Larger items consume more RCUs. Ensure that your items fit within the 4 KB limit to maximize the number of reads per RCU.

- **Caching**: Implement caching strategies to reduce the number of read requests to DynamoDB, which can help lower RCU requirements.

### 3.3.2 Write Capacity Units (WCUs)

WCUs represent the provisioned capacity for writing data to your DynamoDB table. Each WCU allows for one write per second for items up to 1 KB in size. If your items are larger, they will consume more WCUs. Similar to RCUs, you specify the maximum number of writes per second your table can handle when provisioning WCUs.

When provisioning WCUs, consider these factors:

- **Write Patterns**: Understand your application's write patterns. Provision WCUs based on the number of write operations your application performs per second.

- **Item Size**: Keep item sizes as small as possible to maximize the number of writes per WCU.

- **Batch Writes**: Use batch write operations to group multiple write requests into a single request, reducing the number of WCUs consumed.

### 3.3.3 Dynamic Scaling

DynamoDB offers dynamic scaling, which allows your table to automatically adjust its provisioned RCUs and WCUs based on actual usage. This feature is available in the provisioned capacity mode.

With dynamic scaling, you no longer need to manually provision RCUs and WCUs. Instead, DynamoDB monitors your table's usage and adjusts the capacity to meet the demand, ensuring that your application continues to perform optimally without overprovisioning.

### 3.3.4 Monitoring Capacity

To monitor the capacity usage of your DynamoDB table, you can utilize Amazon CloudWatch, a monitoring service provided by AWS. CloudWatch provides metrics and alarms that help you track and manage your RCUs and WCUs effectively.

By setting up CloudWatch alarms, you can receive notifications when your capacity usage exceeds certain thresholds, allowing you to take action to avoid performance issues or unexpected cost overruns.

Understanding and properly provisioning RCUs and WCUs is essential for optimizing the performance and cost-effectiveness of your DynamoDB tables. Whether you choose to provision capacity manually or leverage dynamic scaling, monitoring your capacity usage and adjusting as needed is a critical part of managing your DynamoDB resources effectively. In the upcoming sections, we will explore additional concepts such as secondary indexes, data types, and best practices for modeling your data in DynamoDB.

## 3.4 Indexes in DynamoDB: LSI and GSI

Indexes play a crucial role in enhancing the query performance and flexibility of your DynamoDB tables. DynamoDB offers two types of indexes: Local Secondary Indexes (LSIs) and Global Secondary Indexes (GSIs). Let's explore these index types and understand when and how to use them.

### 3.4.1 Local Secondary Indexes (LSIs)

LSIs are secondary indexes that have the same partition key as the base table but a different sort key. They are limited to the same partition as the base table, which means LSIs are suitable for queries that retrieve data within the same partition.

Use cases for LSIs include:

- **Querying Data within a Partition**: When you need to perform range queries or filter data within a specific partition, LSIs can improve query performance by providing an alternative sort key.

- **Reducing Query Costs**: LSIs can help reduce the number of read capacity units (RCUs) consumed when querying the table, as they enable more efficient filtering.

- **Minimizing Data Transfer**: LSIs allow you to retrieve a subset of data from a single partition, reducing data transfer costs.

### 3.4.2 Global Secondary Indexes (GSIs)

GSIs are secondary indexes with a different partition key and sort key from the base table. They are not limited to the same partition as the base table, making them suitable for queries that span multiple partitions.

GSIs are valuable when:

- **Querying Data Across Partitions**: GSIs enable efficient querying of data across all partitions, making them suitable for scenarios where data needs to be retrieved globally.

- **Diverse Query Patterns**: If your application has diverse query patterns that don't align with the base table's primary key, GSIs allow you to create indexes tailored to specific query requirements.

- **Aggregating Data**: GSIs can aggregate data across partitions, facilitating queries that involve data from multiple items.

### 3.4.3 Creating and Managing Indexes

To create LSIs and GSIs for your DynamoDB table, you can define them when creating the table or add them later through the AWS Management Console or SDKs. Each index requires specifying the index name, partition key, and sort key (if applicable).

Once created, indexes are automatically maintained by DynamoDB as you add, update, or delete items in the base table. You don't need to manage index maintenance manually.

### 3.4.4 Example Use Case

Consider a DynamoDB table that stores order information for an e-commerce platform. The table's primary key could be composed of the partition key CustomerId and the sort key OrderId. However, you also have specific query requirements, such as retrieving all orders by a specific ProductID or filtering orders by OrderStatus.

In this scenario, you can create GSIs to address these query patterns:

- GSI1: ProductID as the partition key and OrderId as the sort key.
- GSI2: OrderStatus as the partition key.

With these GSIs, you can efficiently query orders by product or status without affecting the base table's primary key structure.

### 3.4.5 Considerations and Best Practices

When using indexes in DynamoDB, keep the following considerations in mind:

- Indexes come with additional storage and write costs, so carefully plan and evaluate the indexes you need to create.
- Be mindful of the number of indexes per table, as there is a limit.
- Choose index key attributes wisely to align with your query patterns and access requirements.
- Understand the trade-offs between LSIs and GSIs and choose the appropriate index type for your use case.

• Monitor and manage index performance to ensure they continue to meet your application's requirements.

Indexes provide flexibility and enhanced query capabilities in DynamoDB, allowing you to optimize data retrieval based on various access patterns. Properly designed indexes can significantly improve the efficiency of your database queries. In the following sections, we will explore data types, data modeling best practices, and advanced querying techniques to further enhance your DynamoDB skills.

---

## 3.5 Data Types and Best Practices

In Amazon DynamoDB, understanding data types and best practices for data modeling is crucial for designing efficient and performant database schemas. DynamoDB supports various data types for attributes, and how you use these types can impact your application's performance and cost. Let's delve into data types and best practices in DynamoDB.

### 3.5.1 Data Types

DynamoDB offers a range of data types to represent different types of data in your items:

• **Scalar Types**: These are single-value data types and include:

– String: Textual data.

– Number: Numeric data (integer or floating-point).

– Boolean: True or false values.

– Binary: Binary data, often used for images or documents.

– Null: Represents a null value.

• **Set Types**: These data types can represent multiple values of the same data type without duplicates. Set types include:

– String Set: A set of strings.

– Number Set: A set of numbers.

– Binary Set: A set of binary values.

• **Document Types**: These data types represent complex structures and include:

– List: An ordered list of elements.

– Map: An unordered collection of key-value pairs.

When choosing data types for your attributes, consider the nature of the data and how it will be used. Keep in mind that smaller attribute sizes can help reduce the cost of read and write operations in DynamoDB.

### 3.5.2 Best Practices for Data Modeling

Effective data modeling in DynamoDB involves designing your schema to align with your application's query patterns and access requirements. Here are some best practices for data modeling:

• **Normalize or Denormalize**: Choose between normalizing (splitting data into multiple tables) or denormalizing (combining data into a single table) based on your query patterns. Normalization can reduce storage costs but may require more complex queries, while denormalization can simplify queries but increase storage costs.

• **Use Composite Primary Keys**: When designing your primary key, consider using composite keys (partition key and sort key) to optimize query performance. This allows you to efficiently query and sort data.

• **Optimize for Query Patterns**: Analyze your application's query patterns and design your schema to optimize for the most common and performance-critical queries.

• **Leverage Secondary Indexes**: Utilize Local Secondary Indexes (LSIs) and Global Secondary Indexes (GSIs) to support additional query patterns without affecting the base table's primary key structure.

• **Choose the Right Data Types**: Select appropriate data types for your attributes to minimize storage and optimize query performance. For example, use number types for numerical data and string types for textual data.

• **Minimize Attribute Size**: Keep attribute sizes as small as possible to reduce the cost of read and write operations. Avoid storing large binary objects in DynamoDB; consider using Amazon S3 for that purpose.

• **Use Batch Operations**: Take advantage of batch write and batch get operations to efficiently read and write multiple items in a single request, reducing the number of requests and improving performance.

- **Implement Caching**: Use caching solutions like Amazon DynamoDB Accelerator (DAX) to reduce the load on DynamoDB and improve response times for frequently accessed data.

- **Monitor and Optimize**: Continuously monitor your DynamoDB usage, including capacity units, query performance, and costs. Adjust your schema and provisioned capacity based on usage patterns.

Effective data modeling is a critical aspect of building efficient and cost-effective applications with DynamoDB. By carefully designing your schema, selecting the right data types, and optimizing for query patterns, you can make the most of DynamoDB's capabilities while ensuring high performance and low costs. In the upcoming chapters, we will explore CRUD operations, advanced querying techniques, and application integration with DynamoDB.

# Chapter 4: Data Modeling in DynamoDB

## 4.1 Designing Efficient Tables

Designing efficient tables in Amazon DynamoDB is a critical step in ensuring the performance and scalability of your database. Effective table design involves making decisions about the schema, primary keys, and attributes that will best support your application's query patterns. Let's explore key considerations and best practices for designing tables in DynamoDB.

### 4.1.1 Understand Your Query Patterns

Before creating a table in DynamoDB, it's essential to thoroughly understand the query patterns of your application. Identify the types of queries your application will perform, such as:

- Retrieving items based on specific attributes (e.g., customer ID, product ID).
- Scanning for items with certain characteristics (e.g., all orders within a date range).
- Aggregating data (e.g., calculating the average rating of products).

By understanding these query patterns, you can design your table to optimize for the most common and performance-critical operations.

### 4.1.2 Choose the Right Primary Key

The primary key of your DynamoDB table consists of one or two attributes: the partition key and the optional sort key. Choosing the right primary key is crucial for efficient data access. Consider the following guidelines:

- **Partition Key**: Select a partition key that evenly distributes data and aligns with your primary query patterns. Avoid using attributes with high cardinality (e.g., timestamps) as the partition key, as this can create hot partitions.

- **Sort Key**: If your queries involve range-based operations (e.g., retrieving items within a date range), use a sort key to facilitate these queries. The sort key enables efficient sorting and filtering of items within the same partition.

### 4.1.3 Normalize or Denormalize Data

Decide whether to normalize (splitting data into multiple tables) or denormalize (combining data into a single table) your data based on your query patterns and access requirements. Normalization can reduce storage costs but may require complex queries and multiple round trips to retrieve related data. Denormalization simplifies queries but increases storage costs.

### 4.1.4 Use Composite Primary Keys

Composite primary keys, consisting of both partition and sort keys, allow you to efficiently query and sort data within your DynamoDB table. This is especially useful when your queries involve multiple criteria or require sorting.

### 4.1.5 Avoid Overuse of Secondary Indexes

While secondary indexes (LSIs and GSIs) can support additional query patterns, overusing them can lead to increased storage costs and maintenance overhead. Use secondary indexes judiciously, focusing on the most important and frequently used query patterns.

### 4.1.6 Choose Data Types Wisely

Select appropriate data types for your attributes to minimize storage costs and optimize query performance. Avoid using large data types for attributes that could be represented more efficiently.

### 4.1.7 Implement Caching Strategies

Consider implementing caching solutions like Amazon DynamoDB Accelerator (DAX) to reduce the load on DynamoDB and improve response times for frequently accessed data.

### 4.1.8 Monitor and Iterate

After implementing your DynamoDB table, monitor its performance, capacity usage, and query patterns. Be prepared to iterate on your table design as your application evolves and usage patterns change.

Effective table design in DynamoDB is a combination of understanding your application's query patterns, choosing the right primary key, optimizing for efficiency, and continuous monitoring and refinement. By following best practices and making informed design decisions, you can create DynamoDB tables that provide high-performance and scalable data storage for your applications. In the following sections of this chapter, we will explore various data modeling concepts, including handling relationships, managing large items, and advanced modeling techniques.

## 4.2 Relationships: One-to-One, One-to-Many, Many-to-Many

Effective data modeling in Amazon DynamoDB often involves handling relationships between items in your database. These relationships can vary in complexity, from simple one-to-one relationships to more intricate many-to-many associations. Understanding how to represent and manage these relationships is essential for designing a well-structured database schema. In this section, we'll explore different types of relationships and strategies for modeling them in DynamoDB.

### 4.2.1 One-to-One Relationships

A one-to-one relationship exists when each item in one table is related to exactly one item in another table. In DynamoDB, you can represent one-to-one relationships by including attributes from one table in another. This approach simplifies data access but may increase storage costs, especially if the attributes are sparsely populated.

Consider an example where you have a "User" table and a "Profile" table. Each user has a single profile, and you can include profile attributes as attributes within the "User" table. This allows you to retrieve a user's profile data without additional queries.

```
{
"UserID": "123",
"Username": "john_doe",
"Email": "john@example.com",
"Profile": {
```

"FirstName": "John",

"LastName": "Doe",

"Bio": "Software Engineer",

"Location": "New York"

}

}

### 4.2.2 One-to-Many Relationships

In a one-to-many relationship, each item in one table can be associated with one or more items in another table. To model one-to-many relationships in DynamoDB, you can use various strategies, including:

- **Nested Items**: Store related items as nested structures within an attribute. For example, in an e-commerce application, each "Order" item may contain a list of "Product" items ordered by the customer.

{

"OrderID": "987654",

"CustomerID": "123",

"Products": [

{

"ProductID": "P001",

"Name": "Product A",

"Quantity": 2

},

{

"ProductID": "P002",

"Name": "Product B",

"Quantity": 3

}

]

}

- **Reference IDs**: Use reference IDs to link related items. For example, a "Comment" item in a blogging application can reference the "Post" it belongs to using a "PostID" attribute.

{

"CommentID": "C001",

"Text": "Great post!",

"PostID": "P123"

}

### 4.2.3 Many-to-Many Relationships

Handling many-to-many relationships in DynamoDB can be more complex. Typically, you use an intermediary table (junction table) to represent these relationships. Consider a scenario where you have

"Students" and "Courses." Multiple students can enroll in multiple courses, creating a many-to-many relationship. To model this, you can create a "StudentCourse" table with references to both students and courses.

```
{
"StudentCourseID": "SC001",
"StudentID": "S123",
"CourseID": "C456"
}
```

By creating and managing an intermediary table, you can efficiently query and maintain many-to-many relationships.

### 4.2.4 Choosing the Right Modeling Approach

When modeling relationships in DynamoDB, consider the following factors:

- Query Patterns: Analyze how you will access and query related data. Choose a modeling approach that aligns with your application's query patterns.
- Storage Costs: Be mindful of storage costs, especially when using nested structures or duplicating data to represent relationships.
- Data Consistency: Ensure data consistency by carefully handling updates and deletions when relationships change.

- Query Performance: Optimize your table design to facilitate efficient querying of related data.

Modeling relationships is a critical aspect of designing DynamoDB schemas. Understanding the nature of the relationships in your data and choosing the appropriate modeling approach can lead to a well-organized and efficient database structure. In the subsequent sections, we will explore additional data modeling techniques, handling large items, and advanced modeling strategies.

## 4.3 Handling Large Items and Overflows

In Amazon DynamoDB, each item you store in a table has a maximum size limit of 400 KB. While this size is sufficient for many use cases, there are situations where you may need to work with larger data. Handling large items and overflows in DynamoDB involves strategies and techniques to manage and retrieve data that exceeds the size limit of a single item.

### 4.3.1 Challenges with Large Items

When dealing with large items in DynamoDB, several challenges can arise:

1. **Size Limitation**: The maximum item size of 400 KB may not accommodate large documents, images, or other data types.
2. **Cost Considerations**: Storing and retrieving large items can incur higher storage and read/write costs.
3. **Performance Impact**: Large items can impact query performance, especially if they are frequently accessed or require substantial read/write capacity.

To address these challenges, consider the following strategies:

### 4.3.2 Using S3 for Large Objects

One common approach for handling large objects in DynamoDB is to store the object in Amazon Simple Storage Service (S3) and store a reference to the S3 object in DynamoDB. This allows you to efficiently manage large files while keeping the DynamoDB item size within limits.

For example, if you have a DynamoDB table for storing product information and need to include high-resolution images, you can store the images in S3 and include an S3 URL or object key in the DynamoDB item.

```
{
"ProductID": "123",
"Name": "Product A",
"Description": "Lorem ipsum...",
"ImageURL": "https://s3.amazonaws.com/my-bucket/images/product-a.jpg"
}
```

This approach decouples the storage of large objects from DynamoDB, reducing storage and read/write costs and improving query performance.

### 4.3.3 Data Partitioning

If you have large items that are near the 400 KB size limit, consider partitioning the data into smaller, manageable chunks. You can store these chunks as separate items in DynamoDB and use a common identifier or sequence to link them together.

For example, if you have large textual documents, split the document into smaller sections or paragraphs and store each section as a separate item. Use a document ID or section number to maintain the order.

### 4.3.4 Compression

Compressing large items before storing them in DynamoDB can help reduce storage costs and improve query performance. You can use standard compression libraries to compress and decompress data as needed.

### 4.3.5 Lazy Loading

For large items that are not frequently accessed, consider implementing a lazy loading strategy. Instead of retrieving the entire large item at once, retrieve only the portions needed for the current operation. This can reduce the amount of data transferred and improve performance.

### 4.3.6 Caching

Implement caching mechanisms to store frequently accessed large items in memory, reducing the need to fetch them from DynamoDB repeatedly. Amazon DynamoDB Accelerator (DAX) is a caching service that can be integrated with DynamoDB to improve the retrieval of frequently accessed data.

### 4.3.7 Monitoring and Optimization

Monitor the performance and cost of handling large items in DynamoDB. Adjust your strategies based on usage patterns and optimize the storage and retrieval of large data as needed.

Handling large items and overflows in DynamoDB requires thoughtful planning and implementation. By leveraging techniques like using S3 for large objects, partitioning data, compression, lazy loading, and caching, you can efficiently manage large data while maintaining the scalability and performance of your DynamoDB tables. In the following sections, we will explore additional data modeling techniques and advanced modeling strategies to further enhance your DynamoDB skills.

## 4.4 Data Normalization vs. Denormalization

Data modeling in Amazon DynamoDB involves making decisions about how to structure your data to best serve your application's needs. One crucial decision is whether to normalize or denormalize your data. These two approaches have distinct advantages and trade-offs, and the choice depends on your specific use case and query patterns.

### 4.4.1 Data Normalization

Data normalization is a database design technique where data is organized into separate tables to reduce data redundancy and maintain data integrity. In a normalized schema, related data is stored in different tables, and relationships are established using foreign keys. This approach is common in traditional relational databases but can also be applied to DynamoDB.

*Advantages of Data Normalization:*

1. **Reduced Data Redundancy**: Normalization eliminates data duplication, leading to lower storage costs and reduced chances of data inconsistencies.
2. **Consistency**: Data is consistent and reliable since updates or changes are made in one place.
3. **Easier Updates**: Updates to data only require modifications in one table, simplifying data maintenance.

*Challenges and Considerations:*

1. **Complex Queries**: Retrieving data often requires joining multiple tables, which can result in complex queries and potentially slower performance.
2. **Increased Query Complexity**: Complex queries may involve multiple requests to retrieve related data, impacting query latency.
3. **Scalability**: Normalized data may not align well with DynamoDB's partitioning model, potentially causing hot partitions.

### 4.4.2 Data Denormalization

Data denormalization, on the other hand, involves combining related data into a single table or item, resulting in reduced query complexity but potential data redundancy. Denormalization can be an effective strategy in DynamoDB, especially when query performance and simplicity are essential.

*Advantages of Data Denormalization:*

1. **Simplified Queries**: Data retrieval becomes more

straightforward as related data is stored together, reducing the need for complex joins.

2. **Faster Queries**: Denormalized data typically leads to faster query performance, especially for read-heavy workloads.
3. **Better Scalability**: Denormalization can align better with DynamoDB's partitioning model, distributing data more evenly.

*Challenges and Considerations:*

1. **Data Redundancy**: Denormalized data may lead to redundancy and increased storage costs, as related data is duplicated.
2. **Consistency**: Managing data consistency becomes more complex as updates may require modifications in multiple places.
3. **Increased Write Complexity**: Updates to denormalized data may involve multiple items, which can complicate write operations.

### 4.4.3 Choosing the Right Approach

The choice between data normalization and denormalization depends on your application's requirements and query patterns. Consider the following factors:

- **Query Patterns**: Analyze how your application accesses data and what query patterns are most critical. Normalize data when complex relationships and consistency are crucial, while denormalize for simplified and faster queries.

- **Data Access Patterns**: Think about how often data is read versus written. Denormalization can be more suitable for read-heavy workloads, while normalization may be preferred for write-heavy workloads.

- **Storage Costs**: Evaluate the trade-off between storage costs and query performance. Normalize data to minimize storage costs but denormalize for improved query performance.

- **Data Consistency**: Consider the level of data consistency required. Normalization typically provides stronger data consistency, while denormalization may require additional mechanisms to maintain consistency.

- **Scalability**: Keep in mind DynamoDB's partitioning model. Denormalization can improve scalability by distributing data more evenly across partitions.

In practice, a hybrid approach that combines elements of both normalization and denormalization may be the most effective. Carefully consider your application's specific needs, and adapt your data modeling strategy accordingly. DynamoDB's flexibility allows you to choose the approach that best suits your use case while optimizing for query performance, data consistency, and cost-efficiency.

---

## 4.5 Advanced Modeling Techniques

In Amazon DynamoDB, advanced modeling techniques can help you optimize your data schema and query patterns to achieve better performance, scalability, and cost-efficiency. These techniques go beyond the basics of data modeling and involve strategies to handle complex use cases effectively. In this section, we will explore some advanced modeling techniques to enhance your DynamoDB skills.

### 4.5.1 Hierarchical Data Structures

Hierarchical data structures are common in applications where data is organized in a tree-like hierarchy. DynamoDB can efficiently model and query hierarchical data using a combination of partition keys and sort keys. For example, consider a file system where directories contain files. You can use a partition key to represent directories and a sort key to represent files within each directory. This allows you to efficiently retrieve files within a specific directory or traverse the hierarchy.

### 4.5.2 Time Series Data

When dealing with time series data, such as logs, sensor readings, or financial transactions, it's essential to design your schema to accommodate high write and query rates. DynamoDB's partitioning model can be leveraged effectively for time series data by using time-based values as part of the partition key. This distributes data across partitions and allows for efficient querying of data within specific time intervals.

### 4.5.3 Versioning and Auditing

To implement versioning and auditing of data in DynamoDB, you can use techniques like item versioning and change tracking. By including version numbers or timestamps in your items, you can track changes and retrieve historical versions of data. This is valuable for maintaining data integrity and auditing purposes.

### 4.5.4 Aggregations and Analytics

DynamoDB can be used to perform simple aggregations and analytics on your data. By designing your schema to store aggregated values or statistics, you can efficiently retrieve summary information without the need for complex processing. Aggregations can be useful for generating reports or dashboards based on DynamoDB data.

### 4.5.5 Graph Data

Modeling graph data in DynamoDB involves representing relationships between nodes and edges efficiently. You can use composite keys and adjacency lists to store graph data. For example, in a social network, each user can be a node, and connections between users can be represented as edges. Efficient traversal and querying of the graph can be achieved with the right schema design.

### 4.5.6 Global Tables

Global Tables is a DynamoDB feature that enables multi-region replication for high availability and disaster recovery. By using Global Tables, you can distribute your data across multiple AWS regions, ensuring that your application remains available even in the event of region-wide failures. This advanced technique requires careful planning and configuration but provides robust data redundancy.

### 4.5.7 Time to Live (TTL) for Data Expiry

DynamoDB supports the Time to Live (TTL) feature, allowing you to automatically expire and delete items after a specified time period. This is useful for managing temporary data or implementing data retention policies without manual intervention.

### 4.5.8 Advanced Indexing

Utilize advanced indexing techniques, such as sparse indexes, composite indexes, or composite projections, to optimize query performance and reduce the number of read/write capacity units consumed. Indexing is a powerful tool for fine-tuning your data access patterns.

### 4.5.9 Adaptive Capacity

DynamoDB's adaptive capacity feature automatically adjusts your provisioned read and write capacity based on the actual usage, allowing you to handle traffic spikes and reduce costs during periods of lower usage. Understanding how adaptive capacity works and designing your schema to benefit from it can lead to more cost-effective operations.

### 4.5.10 Time Series Data Retention

Implementing data retention policies for time series data is essential to avoid unnecessary storage costs. You can use strategies like archiving or purging old data based on timestamps to manage data growth efficiently.

Advanced modeling techniques in DynamoDB require a deep understanding of your application's requirements and usage patterns. By carefully designing your schema, leveraging features like Global Tables and TTL, and optimizing for specific use cases such as hierarchical data structures, time series data, or graph data, you can make the most of DynamoDB's capabilities. These techniques empower you to build highly performant, scalable, and cost-effective applications on the DynamoDB platform.

# Chapter 5: CRUD Operations in DynamoDB

## 5.1 Creating Data: PutItem and BatchWriteItem

In Amazon DynamoDB, creating and managing data is fundamental to building efficient applications. DynamoDB provides several methods for creating, reading, updating, and deleting (CRUD) data. In this chapter, we will explore these operations in detail. We'll start with creating data, focusing on the PutItem and BatchWriteItem operations, which allow you to add new items or update existing ones in your DynamoDB tables.

### 5.1.1 PutItem Operation

The PutItem operation is used to create a new item or completely replace an existing item in a DynamoDB table. It requires specifying the table name and providing the entire item you want to add or replace. If an item with the same primary key already exists, it will be overwritten.

Here's an example of using the PutItem operation to add a new item to a "Books" table:

```
import boto3

# Initialize DynamoDB client

dynamodb = boto3.client('dynamodb')

# Define the table name

table_name = 'Books'
```

```
# Define the item to be added
item = {
'ISBN': {'N': '978-0451450524'},
'Title': {'S': 'Neuromancer'},
'Author': {'S': 'William Gibson'},
'PublicationYear': {'N': '1984'}
}
# Perform the PutItem operation
response = dynamodb.put_item(TableName=table_name, Item=item)
# Check the response for success
if response['ResponseMetadata']['HTTPStatusCode'] == 200:
print('Item added successfully.')
else:
print('Failed to add item.')
```

In this example, we use the boto3 library in Python to interact with DynamoDB. We define the item to be added as a dictionary where the keys represent attribute names, and the values are dictionaries with a data type (e.g., 'S' for string, 'N' for number) and the attribute value.

## 5.1.2 BatchWriteItem Operation

The BatchWriteItem operation allows you to perform multiple PutItem and DeleteItem operations in a single request. This is useful for efficiently adding or deleting multiple items in a table. You can include up to 25 PutItem and DeleteItem requests in a single BatchWriteItem request.

Here's an example of using BatchWriteItem to add multiple items to a "Users" table:

```
import boto3

# Initialize DynamoDB client

dynamodb = boto3.client('dynamodb')

# Define the table name

table_name = 'Users'

# Define the items to be added

items = [

{

'UserID': {'N': '101'},

'Username': {'S': 'john_doe'},

'Email': {'S': 'john@example.com'}

},

{

'UserID': {'N': '102'},
```

```
'Username': {'S': 'jane_smith'},
'Email': {'S': 'jane@example.com'}
}
]
# Prepare batch write requests
batch_write_requests = [
{
'PutRequest': {
'Item': item
}
}
for item in items
]
# Perform the BatchWriteItem operation
response = dynamodb.batch_write_item(
RequestItems={
table_name: batch_write_requests
}
)
# Check the response for success
```

```
if response['ResponseMetadata']['HTTPStatusCode'] == 200:

print('Items added successfully.')

else:

print('Failed to add items.')
```

In this example, we define a list of items to be added and then prepare a list of batch write requests. Each request specifies a PutRequest with the item to be added. The batch_write_item method is used to execute the batch write operation.

### 5.1.3 Error Handling and Considerations

When using PutItem and BatchWriteItem, it's essential to consider error handling and potential issues, such as exceeding capacity limits, encountering item size limitations, or dealing with conditional writes. DynamoDB provides error codes and responses that can help you diagnose and handle these situations effectively.

- **Capacity Considerations**: Be mindful of the provisioned read and write capacity units in your table. Exceeding these limits can lead to throttling and reduced performance. Consider using on-demand capacity mode or auto-scaling to manage capacity dynamically.

- **Conditional Writes**: DynamoDB supports conditional writes, allowing you to specify conditions that must be met for the write operation to succeed. This can help prevent unintentional overwrites of existing data.

- **Item Size**: Ensure that the size of the items you are adding does not exceed DynamoDB's 400 KB limit. Large items may require special handling, such as using Amazon

S3 for storage and referencing the S3 object URL in DynamoDB.

- **Error Handling**: Implement robust error handling in your code to handle scenarios where requests fail. This includes handling rate-limiting errors and handling errors related to conditional writes.

Creating data in DynamoDB is a fundamental operation for building applications. Whether you use the PutItem operation to add individual items or the BatchWriteItem operation to perform bulk writes, understanding how to create data effectively is crucial for a well-functioning DynamoDB application. In the subsequent sections, we will explore reading, updating, and deleting data from DynamoDB tables.

## 5.2 Reading Data: GetItem, Query, and Scan

In Amazon DynamoDB, reading data is a fundamental operation that allows you to retrieve information from your tables. DynamoDB provides several methods for reading data, including GetItem, Query, and Scan. Each of these methods serves different purposes and is suitable for specific use cases. In this section, we will explore these methods and their respective use cases.

### 5.2.1 GetItem Operation

The GetItem operation is used to retrieve a single item from a DynamoDB table based on its primary key. It is the most efficient way to retrieve specific items by their unique identifier. The operation requires specifying the table name and providing the primary key values of the item you want to retrieve.

Here's an example of using the GetItem operation to fetch a book from a "Books" table:

```
import boto3

# Initialize DynamoDB client

dynamodb = boto3.client('dynamodb')

# Define the table name

table_name = 'Books'

# Define the primary key for the item to retrieve

key = {

'ISBN': {'N': '978-0451450524'}

}

# Perform the GetItem operation

response = dynamodb.get_item(

TableName=table_name,

Key=key

)

# Check if the item was found

if 'Item' in response:

item = response['Item']

print(f'Book Title: {item["Title"]["S"]}')

print(f'Author: {item["Author"]["S"]}')
```

```
else:

print('Book not found.')
```

In this example, we specify the table name and provide the primary key values as a dictionary. If the item with the specified primary key exists in the table, the response will contain the item's attributes.

### 5.2.2 Query Operation

The Query operation allows you to retrieve multiple items from a DynamoDB table based on a query condition. It is suitable for situations where you want to retrieve items that match specific criteria, such as items with a specific attribute value or within a certain range of values.

Here's an example of using the Query operation to retrieve all books published in a specific year from a "Books" table:

```
import boto3

# Initialize DynamoDB client

dynamodb = boto3.client('dynamodb')

# Define the table name

table_name = 'Books'

# Define the query condition

query_condition = {

'ExpressionAttributeValues': {

':year': {'N': '2000'}

},
```

```
'KeyConditionExpression': 'PublicationYear = :year',
'TableName': table_name
}
# Perform the Query operation
response = dynamodb.query(**query_condition)
# Check if any items were found
if 'Items' in response:
books = response['Items']
for book in books:
print(f'Book Title: {book["Title"]["S"]}')
else:
print('No books found for the specified year.')
```

In this example, we define the query condition using the ExpressionAttributeValues and KeyConditionExpression parameters. The query method is used to execute the query, and the response contains the matching items.

### 5.2.3 Scan Operation

The Scan operation allows you to retrieve all items from a DynamoDB table without specifying a specific query condition. It is suitable when you need to scan the entire table or when your query condition is not based on the table's primary key.

Here's an example of using the Scan operation to retrieve all books authored by a specific author from a "Books" table:

```
import boto3
# Initialize DynamoDB client
dynamodb = boto3.client('dynamodb')
# Define the table name
table_name = 'Books'
# Define the scan condition
scan_condition = {
'ExpressionAttributeValues': {
':author': {'S': 'William Gibson'}
},
'FilterExpression': 'Author = :author',
'TableName': table_name
}
# Perform the Scan operation
response = dynamodb.scan(**scan_condition)
# Check if any items were found
if 'Items' in response:
books = response['Items']
for book in books:
print(f'Book Title: {book["Title"]["S"]}')
```

else:

print('No books by the specified author found.')

In this example, we define the scan condition using the ExpressionAttributeValues and FilterExpression parameters. The scan method is used to execute the scan operation.

### 5.2.4 Query vs. Scan Considerations

When choosing between the Query and Scan operations, consider the following:

- Use Query when you need to retrieve items based on specific criteria, especially when filtering by primary key attributes. Query is more efficient and consumes fewer read capacity units.

- Use Scan when you need to scan the entire table or when your query condition doesn't involve primary key attributes. Keep in mind that Scan consumes more read capacity units and may be slower for large tables.

- Be cautious when using Scan on large tables, as it can be resource-intensive and impact performance. Consider using Query with appropriate indexes whenever possible.

Reading data from DynamoDB is a crucial part of building applications that rely on the information stored in your tables. Whether you use the efficient GetItem operation for specific item retrieval, the powerful Query operation for querying based on criteria, or the versatile Scan operation for broader searches, understanding when and how to use each method is essential for efficient data access. In the following sections, we will explore updating and deleting data in DynamoDB tables.

# 5.3 Updating Data: UpdateItem

Updating data is a common operation in Amazon DynamoDB when you need to modify existing items in your tables. The UpdateItem operation allows you to make changes to attributes within an item or add new attributes. This section will explore the UpdateItem operation and provide examples of how to use it effectively.

## 5.3.1 Basic Usage of UpdateItem

The UpdateItem operation requires specifying the table name, the primary key of the item to be updated, and an update expression that defines the changes to be made. You can update existing attributes or add new ones using this operation.

Here's a basic example of using UpdateItem to increase the stock quantity of a book in a "Books" table:

```
import boto3

# Initialize DynamoDB client

dynamodb = boto3.client('dynamodb')

# Define the table name

table_name = 'Books'

# Define the primary key for the item to update

key = {

'ISBN': {'N': '978-0451450524'}
```

```
}
# Define the update expression to increase stock quantity
update_expression = 'SET StockQuantity = StockQuantity + :quantity'
# Define the expression attribute values
expression_attribute_values = {
':quantity': {'N': '10'}
}
# Perform the UpdateItem operation
response = dynamodb.update_item(
TableName=table_name,
Key=key,
UpdateExpression=update_expression,
ExpressionAttributeValues=expression_attribute_values
)
# Check if the update was successful
if response['ResponseMetadata']['HTTPStatusCode'] == 200:
print('Stock quantity updated successfully.')
else:
print('Failed to update stock quantity.')
```

In this example, we specify the table name, the primary key of the item to be updated, and the update expression that uses the SET action to increase the StockQuantity attribute by 10 units. The ExpressionAttributeValues parameter provides the values for the expression.

## 5.3.2 Conditional Updates

You can use conditional expressions with the UpdateItem operation to update items based on specific conditions. Conditional updates ensure that the update is performed only if certain conditions are met. This helps prevent unintentional updates and allows for safe and controlled data modifications.

Here's an example of a conditional update using UpdateItem to decrease the stock quantity only if the current quantity is greater than zero:

```
import boto3

# Initialize DynamoDB client

dynamodb = boto3.client('dynamodb')

# Define the table name

table_name = 'Books'

# Define the primary key for the item to update

key = {

'ISBN': {'N': '978-0451450524'}

}

# Define the update expression to decrease stock quantity
```

```
update_expression = (
'SET StockQuantity = StockQuantity - :quantity'
)
# Define the condition expression to ensure quantity is greater than zero
condition_expression = 'StockQuantity > :zero'
# Define the expression attribute values
expression_attribute_values = {
':quantity': {'N': '10'},
':zero': {'N': '0'}
}
# Perform the UpdateItem operation with a conditional expression
response = dynamodb.update_item(
TableName=table_name,
Key=key,
UpdateExpression=update_expression,
ConditionExpression=condition_expression,
ExpressionAttributeValues=expression_attribute_values
)
# Check if the update was successful
if response['ResponseMetadata']['HTTPStatusCode'] == 200:
```

```
print('Stock quantity decreased successfully.')
else:
print('Failed to decrease stock quantity due to condition not met.')
```

In this example, we add a conditional expression to ensure that the update is performed only if the StockQuantity is greater than zero.

## 5.3.3 Removing Attributes

You can also use UpdateItem to remove attributes from items by specifying the REMOVE action in the update expression. This allows you to selectively remove specific attributes while keeping the rest of the item intact.

Here's an example of using UpdateItem to remove the "Price" attribute from a book item:

```
import boto3
# Initialize DynamoDB client
dynamodb = boto3.client('dynamodb')
# Define the table name
table_name = 'Books'
# Define the primary key for the item to update
key = {
'ISBN': {'N': '978-0451450524'}
}
# Define the update expression to remove the "Price" attribute
```

```
update_expression = 'REMOVE Price'

# Perform the UpdateItem operation

response = dynamodb.update_item(

TableName=table_name,

Key=key,

UpdateExpression=update_expression

)

# Check if the update was successful

if response['ResponseMetadata']['HTTPStatusCode'] == 200:

print('Price attribute removed successfully.')

else:

print('Failed to remove Price attribute.')
```

In this example, we use the REMOVE action in the update expression to remove the "Price" attribute from the item.

## 5.3.4 Error Handling and Considerations

When working with the UpdateItem operation, consider the following:

- **Concurrency Control**: DynamoDB supports conditional updates to manage concurrency control. Use conditional expressions to ensure that updates are performed based on specific conditions and to prevent conflicts.

- **Attribute Types**: Ensure that the attribute types in your update expressions match the expected data types in your table's schema. Mismatched data types can lead to errors.

- **Rate Limiting**: Be aware of rate-limiting when performing frequent updates to the same item. DynamoDB imposes rate limits on update operations to prevent excessive load.

- **Expression Size**: Be mindful of the size of your update expressions, as they should not exceed DynamoDB's limits. For large updates, consider using multiple smaller updates.

Updating data in DynamoDB is essential for maintaining the accuracy and relevance of your application's information. The UpdateItem operation provides flexibility in modifying existing items and adding new attributes, allowing you to adapt to changing requirements and conditions. When combined with conditional expressions, it ensures safe and controlled updates to your data. In the following sections, we will explore deleting data and performing conditional operations in DynamoDB.

## 5.4 Deleting Data: DeleteItem and BatchWriteItem

Deleting data from Amazon DynamoDB is an essential operation for managing your tables and ensuring that outdated or unnecessary information is removed. DynamoDB provides two primary methods for deleting data: DeleteItem and BatchWriteItem. This section explores these methods and their use cases.

## 5.4.1 DeleteItem Operation

The DeleteItem operation is used to remove a single item from a DynamoDB table based on its primary key. It allows you to specify the table name and provide the primary key values of the item you want to delete.

Here's an example of using the DeleteItem operation to remove a book from a "Books" table:

```
import boto3

# Initialize DynamoDB client

dynamodb = boto3.client('dynamodb')

# Define the table name

table_name = 'Books'

# Define the primary key for the item to delete

key = {

'ISBN': {'N': '978-0451450524'}

}

# Perform the DeleteItem operation

response = dynamodb.delete_item(

TableName=table_name,

Key=key

)

# Check if the item was successfully deleted
```

```
if response['ResponseMetadata']['HTTPStatusCode'] == 200:

print('Item deleted successfully.')

else:

print('Failed to delete item.')
```

In this example, we specify the table name and provide the primary key values of the item to be deleted. If the item with the specified primary key exists in the table, it will be removed.

### 5.4.2 BatchWriteItem for Batch Deletion

The BatchWriteItem operation, which was previously discussed in the context of adding items, can also be used for batch deletion. You can include multiple DeleteItem requests in a single BatchWriteItem request to delete multiple items in one go.

Here's an example of using BatchWriteItem to delete multiple user records from a "Users" table:

```
import boto3

# Initialize DynamoDB client

dynamodb = boto3.client('dynamodb')

# Define the table name

table_name = 'Users'

# Define the primary keys of the items to delete

keys_to_delete = [

{'UserID': {'N': '101'}},
```

```
{'UserID': {'N': '102'}}
]
# Prepare batch delete requests
batch_delete_requests = [
{
'DeleteRequest': {
'Key': key
}
}
for key in keys_to_delete
]
# Perform the BatchWriteItem operation for deletion
response = dynamodb.batch_write_item(
RequestItems={
table_name: batch_delete_requests
}
)
# Check if the deletion was successful
if response['ResponseMetadata']['HTTPStatusCode'] == 200:
print('Items deleted successfully.')
```

```
else:

print('Failed to delete items.')
```

In this example, we define a list of primary keys for the items to be deleted and prepare batch delete requests using the DeleteRequest format. The batch_write_item method is used to execute the batch deletion.

## 5.4.3 Error Handling and Considerations

When deleting data in DynamoDB, consider the following:

- **Conditional Deletion**: Similar to conditional updates, DynamoDB supports conditional deletions. You can use conditional expressions to specify conditions that must be met for the deletion to occur. This helps prevent accidental deletions.

- **Rate Limiting**: Be aware of rate limits when performing frequent delete operations, especially on the same item. DynamoDB imposes rate limits on delete operations to ensure efficient resource usage.

- **Batch Deletion**: When deleting multiple items using BatchWriteItem, ensure that the total size of the batch request does not exceed DynamoDB's limits. You can include up to 25 delete requests in a single batch.

- **Item Size**: Be mindful of the item size when deleting items. Large items may consume more write capacity units, and excessively large items should be managed carefully.

Deleting data from DynamoDB is a critical aspect of maintaining your tables and ensuring that your database remains efficient and up-to-date. Whether you use the DeleteItem operation to remove individual items or leverage the BatchWriteItem operation for batch deletions, understanding how to delete data effectively is essential. In the following section, we will explore conditional operations in DynamoDB, allowing you to control data modifications based on specific conditions.

---

## 5.5 Conditional Operations and Atomic Counters

Conditional operations in Amazon DynamoDB enable you to perform data modifications based on specific conditions, adding an extra layer of control and ensuring that updates or deletes occur only when certain criteria are met. This section explores the use of conditional expressions in DynamoDB and introduces the concept of atomic counters.

### 5.5.1 Conditional Expressions

Conditional expressions are used to specify conditions that must be satisfied for an update or delete operation to occur. You can use conditional expressions with the UpdateItem and DeleteItem operations to make these operations conditional.

A common use case for conditional expressions is preventing updates or deletions if an item's attribute meets certain criteria. For example, you might want to update an item's status only if it is currently in a specific state.

Here's an example of using a conditional expression with the UpdateItem operation to update an item's status only if it's currently in the "Pending" state:

```
import boto3
# Initialize DynamoDB client
dynamodb = boto3.client('dynamodb')
# Define the table name
table_name = 'Orders'
# Define the primary key for the item to update
key = {
'OrderID': {'N': '12345'}
}
# Define the update expression to change status
update_expression = 'SET Status = :new_status'
# Define the condition expression
condition_expression = 'Status = :current_status'
# Define expression attribute values
expression_attribute_values = {
':new_status': {'S': 'Shipped'},
':current_status': {'S': 'Pending'}
}
# Perform the UpdateItem operation with a conditional expression
response = dynamodb.update_item(
```

```
TableName=table_name,

Key=key,

UpdateExpression=update_expression,

ConditionExpression=condition_expression,

ExpressionAttributeValues=expression_attribute_values

)

# Check if the update was successful

if response['ResponseMetadata']['HTTPStatusCode'] == 200:

print('Status updated successfully.')

else:

print('Failed to update status due to condition not met.')
```

In this example, the ConditionExpression ensures that the status update only occurs if the current status is "Pending."

## 5.5.2 Atomic Counters

Atomic counters are a specific type of conditional update in DynamoDB that are commonly used for scenarios where you need to increment or decrement numeric values within an item atomically. Atomic counters prevent conflicts that might occur in multi-user environments when multiple clients try to update the same item simultaneously.

Here's an example of using an atomic counter to increment a "PageViews" attribute in a "WebPage" item:

```
import boto3
```

```
# Initialize DynamoDB client

dynamodb = boto3.client('dynamodb')

# Define the table name

table_name = 'WebPages'

# Define the primary key for the item to update

key = {

'PageID': {'N': '123'}

}

# Define the update expression to increment page views

update_expression = 'SET PageViews = PageViews + :increment_value'

# Define expression attribute values

expression_attribute_values = {

':increment_value': {'N': '1'}

}

# Perform the UpdateItem operation with an atomic counter

response = dynamodb.update_item(

TableName=table_name,

Key=key,

UpdateExpression=update_expression,

ExpressionAttributeValues=expression_attribute_values
```

```
)

# Check if the update was successful

if response['ResponseMetadata']['HTTPStatusCode'] == 200:

print('PageViews incremented successfully.')

else:

print('Failed to increment PageViews.')
```

In this example, the UpdateExpression uses an atomic counter to increment the "PageViews" attribute by one. DynamoDB ensures that this operation is atomic and does not result in conflicts.

### 5.5.3 Error Handling and Considerations

When using conditional operations and atomic counters in DynamoDB, consider the following:

- **Concurrency Control**: Conditional expressions and atomic counters help manage concurrency control and prevent conflicts when multiple clients attempt to modify the same item simultaneously.

- **Data Types**: Ensure that the attribute types in your expressions match the expected data types in your table's schema. Mismatched data types can lead to errors.

- **Rate Limiting**: Be aware of rate limits when performing frequent conditional updates, especially on the same item. DynamoDB enforces rate limits on these operations to prevent excessive load.

- **Expression Size**: Keep your expressions and attribute values within DynamoDB's size limits. For large updates or complex conditions, consider splitting operations into smaller steps.

Conditional operations and atomic counters enhance the precision and control you have over data modifications in DynamoDB. They are valuable tools for managing concurrent access and ensuring that updates or deletes occur only when specific conditions are met. In the following chapters, we will dive deeper into advanced querying techniques, integration with application code, and performance optimization strategies in DynamoDB.

---

Chapter 6: Advanced Querying Techniques 6.1 Efficient Queries and Scans 6.2 Utilizing Secondary Indexes 6.3 Filtering and Sorting Results 6.4 Pagination in Query Results 6.5 Querying with Expressions

Chapter 7: Integrating with Application Code 7.1 DynamoDB SDKs for Popular Programming Languages 7.2 Setting Up Environment for Development 7.3 Basic CRUD Operations in Code 7.4 Error Handling and Debugging 7.5 Best Practices in Application Integration

---

# Chapter 6: Advanced Querying Techniques

## 6.1 Efficient Queries and Scans

In Amazon DynamoDB, efficient querying and scanning are crucial for retrieving the data you need while minimizing the use of read capacity units. This section explores techniques to optimize your queries and scans, making your DynamoDB usage more cost-effective and performant.

### 6.1.1 Query vs. Scan

Before diving into optimization techniques, it's important to understand the fundamental difference between querying and scanning in DynamoDB:

- **Query**: Querying retrieves items based on their primary key attributes. You specify the primary key values to retrieve specific items. Queries are efficient, cost-effective, and generally quicker.

- **Scan**: Scanning, on the other hand, examines every item in the entire table to filter and retrieve the required data. Scans are less efficient, consume more read capacity, and are slower for large tables.

### 6.1.2 Use Indexes Wisely

DynamoDB provides Local Secondary Indexes (LSIs) and Global Secondary Indexes (GSIs) to enhance query efficiency. When designing your tables, consider the following:

- **LSIs**: Use LSIs for queries that involve range key conditions and need to retrieve a subset of data within a single partition. LSIs are suitable for one-to-many and one-to-few relationships.

- **GSIs**: GSIs are more versatile and suitable for a wide range of query patterns, especially when querying across multiple partitions or for complex queries involving different attributes.

### 6.1.3 Query Projection

Query projection allows you to retrieve only the specific attributes you need, reducing the amount of data read and improving query performance. You can define the attributes to project when creating the table or querying it.

Here's an example of querying with projection using the AWS SDK for Python (Boto3):

```
import boto3

# Initialize DynamoDB client

dynamodb = boto3.client('dynamodb')

# Define the table name

table_name = 'Books'

# Define the query parameters with projection

query_params = {

'TableName': table_name,

'KeyConditionExpression': 'Author = :author',
```

```
'ExpressionAttributeValues': {
':author': {'S': 'Jane Doe'}
},
'ProjectionExpression': 'Title, Genre'
}
# Perform the query
response = dynamodb.query(**query_params)
# Process the query results
for item in response['Items']:
print(f'Title: {item["Title"]["S"]}, Genre: {item["Genre"]["S"]}')
```

In this example, the ProjectionExpression specifies that only the "Title" and "Genre" attributes should be included in the query result, reducing the amount of data transferred and read.

## 6.1.4 Query Filters

Query filters allow you to further refine the results of a query by applying conditions on non-key attributes. Filters are applied after the initial query and can help you avoid scanning unwanted items.

Here's an example of using query filters in a DynamoDB query:

```
import boto3
# Initialize DynamoDB client
dynamodb = boto3.client('dynamodb')
# Define the table name
```

```
table_name = 'Orders'
# Define the query parameters with a filter
query_params = {
'TableName': table_name,
'KeyConditionExpression': 'CustomerID = :customer_id',
'ExpressionAttributeValues': {
':customer_id': {'N': '12345'}
},
'FilterExpression': 'OrderStatus = :status',
'ExpressionAttributeValues': {
':status': {'S': 'Shipped'}
}
}
# Perform the query with a filter
response = dynamodb.query(**query_params)
# Process the filtered results
for item in response['Items']:
print(f'OrderID: {item["OrderID"]["N"]}, Status: {item["OrderStatus"]["S"]}')
```

In this example, the FilterExpression is used to retrieve orders with a specific "OrderStatus."

### 6.1.5 Page Size and Pagination

When dealing with large query results, it's essential to implement pagination to avoid overwhelming your application and consuming excessive read capacity. DynamoDB supports pagination through the LastEvaluatedKey parameter.

Here's an example of using pagination to retrieve all items in a query result:

```
import boto3

# Initialize DynamoDB client

dynamodb = boto3.client('dynamodb')

# Define the table name

table_name = 'Products'

# Initialize variables for pagination

start_key = None

page_size = 10

while True:

# Define the query parameters

query_params = {

'TableName': table_name,

'Limit': page_size,

'ExclusiveStartKey': start_key

}
```

```
# Perform the query
response = dynamodb.scan(**query_params)
# Process the current page of results
for item in response['Items']:
print(f'ProductID: {item["ProductID"]["N"]}, Name: {item["ProductName"]["S"]}')
# Check if there are more pages to retrieve
if 'LastEvaluatedKey' in response:
start_key = response['LastEvaluatedKey']
else:
break
```

In this example, the ExclusiveStartKey parameter is used to continue paginating through the results until no more pages are available.

### 6.1.6 Avoid Scans When Possible

As mentioned earlier, scans should be avoided whenever possible, as they can be resource-intensive and costly. If your query pattern can be met with queries or index scans, prefer those methods.

### 6.1.7 Using Query Profiling

DynamoDB provides a query profiler that helps you analyze the query performance and suggests optimizations. You can enable query profiling in the AWS Management Console to gain insights into query execution times and resource usage.

### 6.1.8 Monitor and Tune Query Performance

Regularly monitor your query performance using Amazon CloudWatch and DynamoDB Streams. Adjust your provisioned capacity or auto-scaling settings based on observed query patterns to ensure optimal performance.

Efficient querying is key to getting the most out of Amazon

## 6.2 Utilizing Secondary Indexes

In Amazon DynamoDB, secondary indexes play a vital role in enhancing query flexibility and optimizing access patterns for your data. While primary keys are essential for retrieving items efficiently, secondary indexes allow you to perform queries based on non-key attributes, which is particularly valuable when you have diverse query requirements.

### 6.2.1 Understanding Secondary Indexes

Secondary indexes in DynamoDB are of two types: Local Secondary Indexes (LSIs) and Global Secondary Indexes (GSIs).

- **Local Secondary Index (LSI)**: An LSI is associated with a table and has the same partition key as the table but a different sort key. LSIs are used to perform queries with range key conditions within a single partition. They are beneficial for scenarios where you need to retrieve a subset of data within a single partition quickly.

- **Global Secondary Index (GSI)**: A GSI is a separate index with its partition and sort keys. GSIs allow for more versatile query patterns, as they can span multiple partitions and support queries on attributes not included in the table's primary key. GSIs are particularly useful for one-to-many or many-to-many relationships and complex query requirements.

### 6.2.2 Choosing Between LSI and GSI

When deciding between LSIs and GSIs, consider the following factors:

- **Query Requirements**: If your query patterns involve range key conditions and can be satisfied within a single partition, LSIs may be suitable. For more diverse or complex queries that span multiple partitions, GSIs are a better choice.

- **Data Distribution**: Consider how data is distributed across partitions. If your data is evenly distributed, LSIs may perform well. If data distribution is skewed or your query patterns are diverse, GSIs can handle such scenarios effectively.

- **Data Model**: Your data model and relationships between entities also influence the choice. For one-to-many or many-to-many relationships, GSIs are often more appropriate.

### 6.2.3 Creating Secondary Indexes

You can create secondary indexes when defining your table's schema or add them to an existing table. When creating a secondary index, you specify its partition and sort key attributes.

Here's an example of creating a Global Secondary Index using the AWS SDK for Python (Boto3):

```
import boto3

# Initialize DynamoDB client

dynamodb = boto3.client('dynamodb')

# Define the table name

table_name = 'Books'

# Define the GSI's partition and sort keys

gsi_key_schema = [

{

'AttributeName': 'Genre',

'KeyType': 'HASH' # Partition key

},

{

'AttributeName': 'Author',

'KeyType': 'RANGE' # Sort key

}

]

# Define the GSI's provisioned throughput

gsi_provisioned_throughput = {

'ReadCapacityUnits': 5,

'WriteCapacityUnits': 5
```

```
}
# Create the Global Secondary Index
dynamodb.update_table(
TableName=table_name,
AttributeDefinitions=[
{
'AttributeName': 'Genre',
'AttributeType': 'S' # Assuming 'Genre' is a string attribute
},
{
'AttributeName': 'Author',
'AttributeType': 'S' # Assuming 'Author' is a string attribute
}
],
GlobalSecondaryIndexUpdates=[
{
'Create': {
'IndexName': 'GenreAuthorIndex',
'KeySchema': gsi_key_schema,
'ProvisionedThroughput': gsi_provisioned_throughput
```

```
}
}
]
)
```

In this example, we're creating a GSI named 'GenreAuthorIndex' with 'Genre' as the partition key and 'Author' as the sort key.

### 6.2.4 Querying with Secondary Indexes

Once you've created a secondary index, you can use it to perform queries based on the index's attributes. DynamoDB handles the indexing and querying efficiently, providing you with fast and targeted results.

Here's an example of querying data using a Global Secondary Index:

```
import boto3

# Initialize DynamoDB client

dynamodb = boto3.client('dynamodb')

# Define the table name and index name

table_name = 'Books'

index_name = 'GenreAuthorIndex'

# Define the query parameters

query_params = {

'TableName': table_name,

'IndexName': index_name,
```

```
'KeyConditionExpression': 'Genre = :genre AND Author = :author',
'ExpressionAttributeValues': {
':genre': {'S': 'Science Fiction'},
':author': {'S': 'Isaac Asimov'}
}
}
# Perform the query using the Global Secondary Index
response = dynamodb.query(**query_params)
# Process the query results
for item in response['Items']:
print(f"Title: {item["Title"]["S"]}, Genre: {item["Genre"]["S"]}, Author: {item["Author"]["S"]}')
```

In this example, we're querying the 'Books' table using the 'GenreAuthorIndex' GSI to retrieve books with a specific genre and author.

## 6.2.5 Updating Data with Secondary Indexes

Keep in mind that when updating or inserting data into a table with secondary indexes, DynamoDB automatically manages the indexing for you. You don't need to manually update the indexes; DynamoDB handles it to ensure data consistency.

## 6.2.6 Monitoring and Optimization

Regularly monitor the performance of your secondary indexes using Amazon CloudWatch and DynamoDB Streams. Adjust the provisioned capacity or auto-scaling settings for your indexes based on observed query patterns to ensure optimal performance.

Effective utilization of secondary indexes can significantly enhance your query capabilities and allow you to efficiently access data based on various attributes, making DynamoDB a powerful and flexible NoSQL database.

## 6.3 Filtering and Sorting Results

In Amazon DynamoDB, filtering and sorting are essential techniques for refining query results. Filters allow you to narrow down the items returned by a query, while sorting lets you order the items based on specific attributes. By applying these techniques strategically, you can retrieve exactly the data you need and present it in a meaningful way.

### 6.3.1 Filtering Data

Filtering in DynamoDB involves specifying conditions that must be met for an item to be included in the query results. Filters are applied after the query is executed, which means that all items matching the query conditions are fetched from the table, and then the filter is applied to the retrieved items.

Here's an example of using filtering in a query using the AWS SDK for Python (Boto3):

```
import boto3

# Initialize DynamoDB client

dynamodb = boto3.client('dynamodb')

# Define the table name
```

```
table_name = 'Books'

# Define the query parameters with a filter

query_params = {

'TableName': table_name,

'KeyConditionExpression': 'Genre = :genre',

'FilterExpression': 'Price < :max_price',

'ExpressionAttributeValues': {

':genre': {'S': 'Science Fiction'},

':max_price': {'N': '20'} # Assuming 'Price' is a numeric attribute

}

}

# Perform the query with filtering

response = dynamodb.query(**query_params)

# Process the filtered results

for item in response['Items']:

print(f'Title: {item["Title"]["S"]}, Genre: {item["Genre"]["S"]}, Price: {item["Price"]["N"]}')
```

In this example, we're querying books in the 'Science Fiction' genre with a price less than $20.

It's important to note that while filtering is useful for refining results, it doesn't affect the query's read capacity units. All items matching the query conditions are read, so be mindful of the cost and performance implications of filtering on large datasets.

### 6.3.2 Sorting Data

Sorting results in DynamoDB is primarily achieved by specifying the 'ScanIndexForward' parameter in your query. By default, results are sorted in ascending order based on the sort key. To reverse the sort order and retrieve items in descending order, set 'ScanIndexForward' to 'False'.

Here's an example of sorting query results:

```
import boto3

# Initialize DynamoDB client

dynamodb = boto3.client('dynamodb')

# Define the table name

table_name = 'Books'

# Define the query parameters with sorting

query_params = {

'TableName': table_name,

'KeyConditionExpression': 'Genre = :genre',

'ExpressionAttributeValues': {

':genre': {'S': 'Mystery'}

},

'ScanIndexForward': False # Sort in descending order
```

```
}

# Perform the query with sorting

response = dynamodb.query(**query_params)

# Process the sorted results

for item in response['Items']:

print(f'Title: {item["Title"]["S"]}, Genre: {item["Genre"]["S"]}, Author: {item["Author"]["S"]}')
```

In this example, we're querying books in the 'Mystery' genre and sorting them in descending order.

### 6.3.3 Combining Filtering and Sorting

You can combine filtering and sorting to retrieve precisely the data you need in the desired order. This allows you to create tailored queries to meet specific application requirements efficiently.

When using both filtering and sorting, remember that filtering is applied after sorting. Therefore, filtering criteria should be considered in conjunction with your query's sort key and partition key for optimal performance.

Filtering and sorting are powerful techniques to help you navigate and present your data effectively in DynamoDB, providing you with flexibility in querying and retrieving items based on your application's needs.

## 6.4 Pagination in Query Results

Pagination is a crucial aspect of working with large datasets in Amazon DynamoDB. When your query results contain more items than can be retrieved in a single request, you'll need to implement pagination to retrieve all the data efficiently. DynamoDB provides mechanisms for handling pagination in query results to ensure you can access all the relevant items.

### 6.4.1 Limit and Pagination Token

In DynamoDB, you can limit the number of items returned in a query by using the 'Limit' parameter. By specifying the maximum number of items you want in a single response, you can control the amount of data retrieved. However, when there are more items available than the limit allows, DynamoDB returns a pagination token in the response.

The pagination token, also known as 'LastEvaluatedKey,' indicates where the next set of results begins. To retrieve the next page of results, you use this token in your subsequent query. This process continues until there are no more pagination tokens, signifying that you have retrieved all the data matching your query.

Here's an example of how to use 'Limit' and the pagination token in a query using the AWS SDK for Python (Boto3):

```
import boto3

# Initialize DynamoDB client

dynamodb = boto3.client('dynamodb')

# Define the table name

table_name = 'Books'

# Initialize variables for pagination

limit = 5 # Maximum items per page
```

```
pagination_token = None

while True:

# Define the query parameters with 'Limit' and pagination token

query_params = {

'TableName': table_name,

'KeyConditionExpression': 'Genre = :genre',

'ExpressionAttributeValues': {

':genre': {'S': 'Fantasy'}

},

'Limit': limit

}

# Add pagination token if available

if pagination_token:

query_params['ExclusiveStartKey'] = pagination_token

# Perform the query

response = dynamodb.query(**query_params)

# Process the query results

for item in response['Items']:

print(f'Title: {item["Title"]["S"]}, Genre: {item["Genre"]["S"]}, Author: {item["Author"]["S"]}')

# Check if there are more pages to retrieve
```

pagination_token = response.get('LastEvaluatedKey', None)

**if not** pagination_token:

**break** *# No more pages to retrieve*

In this example, we're querying books in the 'Fantasy' genre with a limit of 5 items per page and using the pagination token to retrieve subsequent pages.

### 6.4.2 Implementing Pagination in Applications

When implementing pagination in your applications, you need to manage the pagination token, keep track of the pages retrieved, and decide when to stop querying based on the absence of a pagination token. Additionally, you may provide controls for users to navigate between pages, such as "Next" and "Previous" buttons.

Pagination ensures efficient data retrieval and improves the responsiveness of your applications, especially when dealing with large datasets in DynamoDB. By properly implementing pagination, you can provide a seamless experience for users while working with extensive data collections.

---

## 6.5 Querying with Expressions

In Amazon DynamoDB, querying with expressions allows you to perform complex queries and filter results based on various conditions. Expressions provide a flexible way to define the criteria for selecting items from your tables. You can use two types of expressions in DynamoDB: Key Condition Expressions and Filter Expressions.

## 6.5.1 Key Condition Expressions

Key Condition Expressions are used primarily when querying items with specific values in the primary key attributes (partition key and sort key). These expressions determine which items are returned by a query based on the values of these attributes.

Here's an example of using a Key Condition Expression in a query using the AWS SDK for Python (Boto3):

```
import boto3

# Initialize DynamoDB client

dynamodb = boto3.client('dynamodb')

# Define the table name

table_name = 'Books'

# Define the query parameters with a Key Condition Expression

query_params = {

'TableName': table_name,

'KeyConditionExpression': 'Genre = :genre AND ReleaseYear > :year',

'ExpressionAttributeValues': {

':genre': {'S': 'Science Fiction'},

':year': {'N': '2000'}

}

}
```

```
# Perform the query with the Key Condition Expression

response = dynamodb.query(**query_params)

# Process the query results

for item in response['Items']:

print(f'Title: {item["Title"]["S"]}, Genre: {item["Genre"]["S"]}, Year: {item["ReleaseYear"]["N"]}')
```

In this example, we're querying books in the 'Science Fiction' genre released after the year 2000.

## 6.5.2 Filter Expressions

Filter Expressions, on the other hand, are used to filter results after the initial query has been executed. These expressions allow you to refine the results further based on non-key attributes. Filter Expressions are applied to the items retrieved by the query, and only the items that meet the filter criteria are included in the result set.

Here's an example of using a Filter Expression in a query:

```
import boto3

# Initialize DynamoDB client

dynamodb = boto3.client('dynamodb')

# Define the table name

table_name = 'Books'

# Define the query parameters with a Filter Expression

query_params = {
```

```
'TableName': table_name,
'KeyConditionExpression': 'Genre = :genre',
'FilterExpression': 'Price < :max_price',
'ExpressionAttributeValues': {
':genre': {'S': 'Fantasy'},
':max_price': {'N': '30'} # Assuming 'Price' is a numeric attribute
}
}
# Perform the query with the Filter Expression
response = dynamodb.query(**query_params)
# Process the query results
for item in response['Items']:
print(f'Title: {item["Title"]["S"]}, Genre: {item["Genre"]["S"]}, Price: {item["Price"]["N"]}')
```

In this example, we're querying books in the 'Fantasy' genre with a price less than $30 using a Filter Expression.

### 6.5.3 Use Cases for Expressions

Querying with expressions becomes especially useful when you need to perform complex searches or filter data based on specific criteria. You can combine Key Condition Expressions and Filter Expressions to retrieve precisely the data you need from DynamoDB tables, making your queries more efficient and targeted.

Expressions in DynamoDB provide a powerful tool for customizing your queries to match the requirements of your applications, enabling you to retrieve and filter data with precision. When designing queries, consider the data model, access patterns, and the specific attributes you need to filter on to make the most of these expressions.

---

# 7. Integrating with Application Code

## 7.1 DynamoDB SDKs for Popular Programming Languages

To integrate Amazon DynamoDB with your application code, you can use the official SDKs (Software Development Kits) provided by AWS. These SDKs offer convenient libraries and APIs for various programming languages, making it easier to interact with DynamoDB programmatically. In this section, we'll explore the DynamoDB SDKs available for popular programming languages and how to use them to perform common database operations.

### 7.1.1 AWS SDKs

Amazon Web Services (AWS) offers SDKs for a wide range of programming languages, including Python, Java, JavaScript (Node.js), .NET (C#), PHP, Ruby, Go, and more. These SDKs provide language-specific libraries and tools to interact with AWS services, including DynamoDB.

#### *7.1.1.1 AWS SDK for Python (Boto3)*

Boto3 is the official SDK for Python, developed and maintained by AWS. It allows Python developers to interact with various AWS services, including DynamoDB, using a Pythonic and intuitive API.

Here's how to get started with Boto3 for DynamoDB in Python:

```
import boto3

# Initialize DynamoDB client

dynamodb = boto3.client('dynamodb')
```

```
# Define the table name

table_name = 'Books'

# Example: Querying items

response = dynamodb.query(

TableName=table_name,

KeyConditionExpression='Genre = :genre',

ExpressionAttributeValues={

':genre': {'S': 'Fantasy'}

}

)

# Process the query results

for item in response['Items']:

print(f'Title: {item["Title"]["S"]}, Genre: {item["Genre"]["S"]}')
```

### *7.1.1.2 AWS SDK for Java*

The AWS SDK for Java provides comprehensive libraries and tools for Java developers to work with DynamoDB. It includes both low-level and high-level APIs for DynamoDB, allowing you to choose the level of abstraction that suits your needs.

Here's an example of querying items in DynamoDB using the AWS SDK for Java:

```
import software.amazon.awssdk.regions.Region;
```

```
import
software.amazon.awssdk.services.dynamodb.DynamoDbClient;

import software.amazon.awssdk.services.dynamodb.model.*;

public class DynamoDBExample {

public static void main(String[] args) {

// Initialize DynamoDB client

DynamoDbClient dynamoDb = DynamoDbClient.builder()

.region(Region.US_EAST_1)

.build();

// Define the table name

String tableName = "Books";

// Example: Querying items

QueryResponse response =
dynamoDb.query(QueryRequest.builder()

.tableName(tableName)

.keyConditionExpression("Genre = :genre")

.expressionAttributeValues(Map.of(":genre",
AttributeValue.builder().s("Fantasy").build()))

.build());

// Process the query results

for (Map<String, AttributeValue> item : response.items()) {
```

```
System.out.println("Title: " + item.get("Title").s() + ", Genre: " + item.get("Genre").s());

}

// Close the DynamoDB client when done

dynamoDb.close();

}

}
```

These are just two examples of how to use the AWS SDKs for Python and Java with DynamoDB. You can find SDKs for other programming languages on the AWS website and follow the respective documentation to get started.

Using the official SDKs simplifies interactions with DynamoDB and provides robust error handling, authentication, and support for best practices, making it easier to integrate DynamoDB into your applications effectively.

## 7.2 Setting Up Environment for Development

Before you start integrating Amazon DynamoDB with your application code, it's essential to set up your development environment correctly. This ensures that you have all the necessary tools, libraries, and configurations in place to work seamlessly with DynamoDB. In this section, we'll discuss the key steps to set up your development environment for DynamoDB integration.

### 7.2.1 AWS Account and Credentials

First and foremost, you need an AWS account to use DynamoDB and other AWS services. If you don't have an AWS account, you can sign up for one on the AWS website.

Once you have an AWS account, you'll need to configure your credentials for programmatic access to AWS services. AWS uses access keys (Access Key ID and Secret Access Key) to authenticate your requests. You can set up access keys in the AWS Management Console by navigating to the IAM (Identity and Access Management) service and creating a new IAM user with programmatic access. Be sure to securely store your access keys as they grant access to your AWS resources.

### 7.2.2 Installing AWS SDKs

To interact with DynamoDB from your development environment, you'll need to install the appropriate AWS SDK for your chosen programming language. As mentioned earlier, AWS provides SDKs for various languages, including Python, Java, JavaScript, .NET, PHP, Ruby, Go, and more.

You can usually install the AWS SDK for your language using a package manager or by downloading it from the official AWS website. Make sure to follow the installation instructions provided in the SDK's documentation.

### 7.2.3 Configuring AWS SDK

After installing the SDK, you'll need to configure it with your AWS credentials and other settings. The SDK typically allows you to set these configurations either programmatically or through environment variables. Here's an example of configuring the AWS SDK for Python (Boto3):

```
import boto3

# Configure AWS credentials and region

aws_access_key_id = 'your-access-key-id'

aws_secret_access_key = 'your-secret-access-key'

aws_region = 'us-east-1'

# Initialize DynamoDB client with configurations

dynamodb = boto3.client('dynamodb', region_name=aws_region, aws_access_key_id=aws_access_key_id, aws_secret_access_key=aws_secret_access_key)
```

Make sure to replace 'your-access-key-id' and 'your-secret-access-key' with your actual AWS access key and secret access key.

### 7.2.4 Creating a Local Development Environment

For development and testing purposes, it's often helpful to set up a local development environment that mimics DynamoDB. Tools like DynamoDB Local or local testing frameworks for your chosen programming language can simulate DynamoDB operations locally, allowing you to develop and test without incurring AWS costs.

Using a local development environment helps ensure that your code behaves as expected before deploying it to a production AWS environment.

### 7.2.5 Version Control and Code Repository

Consider using version control systems like Git and hosting your code in a code repository, such as GitHub, GitLab, or Bitbucket.

Version control allows you to track changes to your code, collaborate with team members, and roll back to previous versions if needed.

Setting up your development environment properly is a crucial step when integrating DynamoDB with your application code. It ensures that you have the necessary tools, configurations, and security in place to work with DynamoDB effectively. Once your environment is set up, you can proceed to develop, test, and deploy your application with DynamoDB integration.

## 7.3 Basic CRUD Operations in Code

Once you have set up your development environment and configured the AWS SDK for your chosen programming language, you can start performing basic CRUD (Create, Read, Update, Delete) operations on Amazon DynamoDB tables. In this section, we'll explore how to execute these operations using code examples in Python and Java.

### 7.3.1 Create (PutItem)

Creating new items in a DynamoDB table is achieved using the PutItem operation. You provide the item data in the form of JSON-like structures, and DynamoDB adds the item to the specified table.

***Python Example:***

```
import boto3

# Initialize DynamoDB client

dynamodb = boto3.client('dynamodb')
```

```
# Define the table name
table_name = 'Books'
# Define the item to be added
new_item = {
'Title': {'S': 'The Great Gatsby'},
'Author': {'S': 'F. Scott Fitzgerald'},
'Genre': {'S': 'Classic Literature'},
'PublicationYear': {'N': '1925'}
}
# Add the item to the table
response = dynamodb.put_item(
TableName=table_name,
Item=new_item
)
print("Item added successfully!")
```

***Java Example:***

```
import software.amazon.awssdk.regions.Region;
import
software.amazon.awssdk.services.dynamodb.DynamoDbClient;
import software.amazon.awssdk.services.dynamodb.model.*;
```

```
public class DynamoDBExample {

public static void main(String[] args) {

// Initialize DynamoDB client

DynamoDbClient dynamoDb = DynamoDbClient.builder()

.region(Region.US_EAST_1)

.build();

// Define the table name

String tableName = "Books";

// Define the item to be added

Item newItem = Item.builder()

.put("Title", "The Great Gatsby")

.put("Author", "F. Scott Fitzgerald")

.put("Genre", "Classic Literature")

.put("PublicationYear", 1925)

.build();

// Add the item to the table

PutItemResponse response = dynamoDb.putItem(PutItemRequest.builder()

.tableName(tableName)

.item(newItem)

.build());
```

```
System.out.println("Item added successfully!");

}

}
```

## 7.3.2 Read (GetItem)

Reading items from a DynamoDB table can be done using the GetItem operation. You specify the primary key of the item you want to retrieve, and DynamoDB returns the item's attributes.

***Python Example:***

```
import boto3

# Initialize DynamoDB client

dynamodb = boto3.client('dynamodb')

# Define the table name

table_name = 'Books'

# Define the primary key of the item to retrieve

key = {'Title': {'S': 'The Great Gatsby'}}

# Retrieve the item from the table

response = dynamodb.get_item(

TableName=table_name,

Key=key

)
```

```
# Extract and print the item data

item = response.get('Item')

if item:

print("Item found:")

for key, value in item.items():

print(f"{key}: {list(value.values())[0]}")

else:

print("Item not found.")
```

***Java Example:***

```
import software.amazon.awssdk.regions.Region;

import
software.amazon.awssdk.services.dynamodb.DynamoDbClient;

import software.amazon.awssdk.services.dynamodb.model.*;

public class DynamoDBExample {

public static void main(String[] args) {

// Initialize DynamoDB client

DynamoDbClient dynamoDb = DynamoDbClient.builder()

.region(Region.US_EAST_1)

.build();

// Define the table name
```

```
String tableName = "Books";

// Define the primary key of the item to retrieve

Key key = Key.builder()

.partitionValue("The Great Gatsby")

.build();

// Retrieve the item from the table

GetItemResponse response = dynamoDb.getItem(GetItemRequest.builder()

.tableName(tableName)

.key(key)

.build());

// Extract and print the item data

if (response.hasItem()) {

System.out.println("Item found:");

for (String keyName : response.item().keySet()) {

System.out.println(keyName + ": " + response.item().get(keyName));

}

} else {

System.out.println("Item not found.");

}
```

```
}
}
```

These code examples demonstrate how to perform basic Create and Read operations in DynamoDB using Python and Java SDKs. Similar operations can be executed for Update and Delete as well, following the DynamoDB SDK's respective methods.

# 7.4 Error Handling and Debugging

In any software development project, error handling and debugging are essential aspects of ensuring the reliability and correctness of your code. When working with Amazon DynamoDB, you need to be prepared to handle various types of errors that can occur during database operations. This section covers error handling best practices and debugging techniques when interacting with DynamoDB using SDKs like Python and Java.

## 7.4.1 Error Handling Best Practices

*1. Use Exception Handling:*

- When interacting with DynamoDB using SDKs, always use try-catch blocks or exception handling mechanisms provided by the programming language. This helps in gracefully handling errors and prevents your application from crashing due to unhandled exceptions.

*2. Handle Expected Errors:*

- Different DynamoDB operations can result in specific error types, such as conditional check failures or resource not found errors. Identify the expected errors for each operation and handle them accordingly.

### 3. *Exponential Backoff and Retry:*

- DynamoDB might return temporary errors due to capacity limitations or network issues. Implement exponential backoff and retry mechanisms to handle these transient errors. SDKs often provide built-in retry functionality.

### 4. *Logging:*

- Implement robust logging to capture error details. Logging is crucial for diagnosing issues during development and production. Log relevant information, including error codes, error messages, and timestamps.

### 5. *Throttling:*

- DynamoDB imposes rate limits on requests to prevent abuse. Monitor and handle throttling errors (HTTP status code 400 with "ProvisionedThroughputExceededException" or "ThrottlingException") by adjusting your provisioned capacity or implementing retry logic.

### 7.4.2 Debugging Techniques

*1. Use Debuggers:*

• Most modern IDEs and development environments provide debugging tools. Use these tools to step through your code, set breakpoints, and inspect variables to identify issues in your DynamoDB interactions.

*2. Query and Scan Debugging:*

• When working with query and scan operations, test your query expressions or filter conditions separately to ensure they return the expected results before integrating them into your application.

*3. Monitor AWS CloudWatch Metrics:*

• DynamoDB emits various CloudWatch metrics that can help you monitor the health and performance of your tables. Configure alarms to get notified of issues like high error rates or provisioned throughput exceeded.

*4. AWS SDK Logging:*

• Enable AWS SDK logging to capture detailed information about the requests and responses sent to DynamoDB. This can be useful for diagnosing issues with your API calls.

### 7.4.3 Python Example - Error Handling

```
import boto3
```

```
from botocore.exceptions import ClientError

# Initialize DynamoDB client

dynamodb = boto3.client('dynamodb')

# Define the table name

table_name = 'Books'

try:

# Attempt to read an item

response = dynamodb.get_item(

TableName=table_name,

Key={'Title': {'S': 'Nonexistent Book'}}

)

item = response.get('Item')

if item:

print("Item found:")

print(item)

else:

print("Item not found.")

except ClientError as e:

if e.response['Error']['Code'] == 'ResourceNotFoundException':

print("Table not found.")
```

```
elif e.response['Error']['Code'] == 'ProvisionedThroughputExceededException':

print("Provisioned throughput exceeded. Implement retry logic.")

else:

print("An unexpected error occurred:", e)
```

### 7.4.4 Java Example - Error Handling

```
import software.amazon.awssdk.regions.Region;

import software.amazon.awssdk.services.dynamodb.DynamoDbClient;

import software.amazon.awssdk.services.dynamodb.model.*;

public class DynamoDBExample {

public static void main(String[] args) {

// Initialize DynamoDB client

DynamoDbClient dynamoDb = DynamoDbClient.builder()

.region(Region.US_EAST_1)

.build();

// Define the table name

String tableName = "Books";

try {

// Attempt to read an item
```

```
GetItemResponse response = dynamoDb.getItem(GetItemRequest.builder()
.tableName(tableName)
.key(Key.builder()
.partitionValue("Nonexistent Book")
.build())
.build());
if (response.hasItem()) {
System.out.println("Item found:");
System.out.println(response.item());
} else {
System.out.println("Item not found.");
}
} catch (DynamoDbException e) {
if (e instanceof ResourceNotFoundException) {
System.out.println("Table not found.");
} else if (e instanceof ProvisionedThroughputExceededException) {
System.out.println("Provisioned throughput exceeded. Implement retry logic.");
} else {
```

```
System.out.println("An unexpected error occurred: " + e.getMessage());
}
}
}
}
```

These examples illustrate error handling and debugging techniques when using DynamoDB SDKs in Python and Java. Implementing proper error handling and debugging practices is crucial for building robust and reliable applications that interact with DynamoDB.

## 7.5 Best Practices in Application Integration

Integrating Amazon DynamoDB into your application requires careful consideration of various best practices to ensure optimal performance, scalability, and reliability. In this section, we'll explore some key best practices for integrating DynamoDB into your applications effectively.

### 7.5.1 Use Proper AWS SDKs

When integrating DynamoDB into your application, use the official AWS SDKs provided by Amazon Web Services for your programming language. AWS SDKs simplify the process of interacting with DynamoDB by providing pre-built functions and classes tailored for DynamoDB operations. These SDKs also handle authentication and error handling, reducing the complexity of your code.

### 7.5.2 Implement Retry and Exponential Backoff

To handle transient errors and throttling issues gracefully, implement retry logic with exponential backoff. Many AWS SDKs offer built-in retry mechanisms, so you don't have to implement this from scratch. Configuring retries ensures that your application can recover from temporary failures without compromising user experience.

### 7.5.3 Use DynamoDB Streams for Real-time Processing

DynamoDB Streams allow you to capture changes to your tables in real-time. By integrating DynamoDB Streams into your application, you can react to data changes immediately and trigger actions, such as updating caches or sending notifications. This feature is valuable for building event-driven and responsive applications.

### 7.5.4 Leverage AWS Lambda for Serverless Architectures

AWS Lambda enables you to create serverless applications that respond to DynamoDB events. You can configure Lambda functions to execute code in response to changes in your DynamoDB tables. This serverless architecture is cost-effective and scales automatically, making it suitable for various use cases.

### 7.5.5 Implement Data Validation and Sanitization

Ensure that data entering your DynamoDB tables is properly validated and sanitized to prevent security vulnerabilities and data corruption. Implement input validation and data transformation logic in your application code to maintain data integrity.

### 7.5.6 Cache Frequently Accessed Data

To reduce the load on DynamoDB and improve application performance, consider implementing caching mechanisms like Amazon DynamoDB Accelerator (DAX) or in-memory caches. Caching can significantly reduce the number of DynamoDB requests for frequently accessed data.

### 7.5.7 Implement Rate Limiting and Throttling

To prevent excessive requests to DynamoDB, implement rate limiting mechanisms within your application. This helps protect your DynamoDB tables from being overwhelmed by traffic spikes. AWS Identity and Access Management (IAM) policies and Amazon API Gateway can be used to enforce rate limits.

### 7.5.8 Monitor and Analyze Performance

Implement monitoring and analytics solutions to gain insights into the performance and health of your DynamoDB tables. AWS CloudWatch and third-party monitoring tools can help you track metrics, set up alarms, and identify performance bottlenecks.

### 7.5.9 Implement Security Best Practices

Follow AWS security best practices to protect your DynamoDB data. Implement access control using AWS Identity and Access Management (IAM) roles and policies. Enable encryption at rest and in transit to safeguard sensitive information.

### 7.5.10 Plan for Scalability and Disaster Recovery

Design your application architecture with scalability and disaster recovery in mind. Utilize DynamoDB's auto-scaling capabilities to handle varying workloads and implement backup and restore strategies to ensure data availability in case of unexpected events.

### 7.5.11 Test and Optimize

Regularly test your application's integration with DynamoDB to identify areas for optimization. Monitor performance, review query patterns, and fine-tune your data model, indexes, and queries to achieve the best possible performance and cost-efficiency.

By following these best practices, you can ensure a seamless integration of Amazon DynamoDB into your applications while maintaining high performance, reliability, and security. DynamoDB's flexibility and scalability make it a powerful choice for a wide range of use cases, from small-scale applications to large, high-traffic systems.

# Chapter 8: Performance Optimization

## 8.1 Understanding and Managing Throughput

Performance optimization in Amazon DynamoDB is crucial to ensure your applications run smoothly and cost-effectively. One of the key aspects of performance optimization is understanding and managing throughput effectively. In this section, we'll delve into the concept of throughput in DynamoDB and explore strategies for optimizing it.

### Understanding Throughput in DynamoDB

In DynamoDB, throughput is the measure of the capacity that a table or index can provide for read and write operations. DynamoDB offers two modes for throughput provisioning:

1. **Provisioned Throughput:** In this mode, you specify the read and write capacity units your table or index should have. You prepay for the provisioned capacity on an hourly basis. Provisioned throughput is suitable for applications with predictable workloads.
2. **On-Demand Mode:** In this mode, DynamoDB automatically manages the read and write capacity for your table or index. You are charged for the actual usage on a per-request basis. On-demand mode is ideal for applications with variable or unpredictable workloads.

## Optimizing Provisioned Throughput

### *8.1.1 Right-Sizing Provisioned Capacity*

To optimize provisioned throughput, it's essential to right-size your capacity. Start by monitoring your application's read and write patterns using Amazon CloudWatch metrics. Adjust the provisioned capacity based on actual usage to avoid over-provisioning or under-provisioning.

### *8.1.2 Utilizing Auto Scaling*

DynamoDB offers Auto Scaling, a feature that automatically adjusts your provisioned capacity based on workload changes. Enable Auto Scaling to ensure your tables and indexes can handle traffic spikes without manual intervention.

### *8.1.3 Efficiently Distributing Workloads*

Distribute your workloads evenly across partitions to avoid hot partitions. Hot partitions can lead to unevenly distributed read and write requests, causing performance bottlenecks. Use random or semi-random partition keys to achieve even distribution.

### *8.1.4 Monitoring and Alarming*

Set up CloudWatch alarms to monitor your provisioned throughput usage. Alarms can alert you when your utilization approaches or exceeds the provisioned capacity, allowing you to take timely actions.

## Optimizing On-Demand Mode

### *8.1.5 Monitoring Costs in On-Demand Mode*

While On-Demand mode offers flexibility, it's essential to monitor your costs closely. The pay-as-you-go model can lead to unpredictable billing if your application experiences unexpected spikes in traffic.

### *8.1.6 Switching to Provisioned Mode*

If your application's workload becomes predictable over time, consider switching to provisioned mode. This can provide cost savings compared to the pay-as-you-go model while maintaining performance.

## Balancing Cost and Performance

Optimizing throughput in DynamoDB is a delicate balance between cost and performance. It requires continuous monitoring, capacity adjustments, and understanding your application's workload patterns. By following the strategies mentioned above, you can ensure that your DynamoDB tables and indexes deliver the required performance while optimizing costs.

# 8.2 Read/Write Capacity Mode: On-Demand vs. Provisioned

In DynamoDB, you have the flexibility to choose between two read/write capacity modes: On-Demand and Provisioned. Each mode has its characteristics, and your choice should align with your application's requirements and workload patterns. In this section, we'll explore the differences between these two modes and when to use them.

## On-Demand Capacity Mode

### *8.2.1 Characteristics*

In On-Demand capacity mode, DynamoDB automatically adjusts your read and write capacity based on the actual traffic your application receives. You are charged per request, making it suitable for applications with variable workloads or those where predicting capacity needs is challenging.

### *8.2.2 Benefits*

- **Cost Efficiency:** On-Demand mode eliminates the need for upfront capacity provisioning. You only pay for the actual requests you make, making it cost-effective for applications with sporadic or unpredictable traffic.

- **Scalability:** DynamoDB scales your capacity up or down instantly in response to changes in traffic. It can handle traffic spikes without manual intervention.

- **Simplified Management:** You don't need to monitor or adjust provisioned capacity; DynamoDB takes care of it for you.

## Provisioned Capacity Mode

### *8.2.3 Characteristics*

In Provisioned capacity mode, you specify the read and write capacity units your table or index should have. You prepay for this capacity on an hourly basis. This mode is ideal for applications with steady and predictable workloads.

### *8.2.4 Benefits*

- **Predictable Costs:** With Provisioned mode, you know your monthly costs in advance, making it suitable for budget-conscious projects.
- **Full Control:** You have granular control over the capacity settings, allowing you to optimize performance for specific workloads.
- **Reserved Capacity:** AWS offers Reserved Capacity options that provide cost savings for long-term commitments.

## When to Use Each Mode

### *8.2.5 Use On-Demand Mode When:*

- Your application has unpredictable or variable workloads.
- You want to eliminate the need for capacity planning and provisioning.

- Cost optimization is a priority, and you are willing to pay for the flexibility of auto-scaling.

*8.2.6 Use Provisioned Mode When:*

- Your application has steady and predictable workloads.

- You want to have full control over capacity settings for optimization.

- Cost predictability is essential, and you are willing to commit to a reserved capacity.

## Switching Between Modes

*8.2.7 Transitioning to On-Demand Mode*

If you initially choose Provisioned mode but later find that your workload becomes more variable, you can easily switch to On-Demand mode without downtime or data migration.

*8.2.8 Transitioning to Provisioned Mode*

Conversely, if you start with On-Demand mode and your workload stabilizes, you can switch to Provisioned mode to optimize costs.

In summary, the choice between On-Demand and Provisioned capacity modes in DynamoDB depends on your application's workload patterns and cost considerations. Both modes have their advantages, and DynamoDB's flexibility allows you to switch between them as your needs evolve.

---

# 8.3 Performance Monitoring with

# CloudWatch

Performance monitoring is crucial to ensure that your DynamoDB tables are operating efficiently and meeting your application's performance requirements. Amazon CloudWatch is a comprehensive monitoring and observability service that allows you to collect and track metrics, collect and monitor log files, and set alarms. In this section, we'll explore how you can use CloudWatch to monitor your DynamoDB resources effectively.

## Metrics for DynamoDB

Amazon CloudWatch provides a variety of metrics for DynamoDB tables, enabling you to monitor key performance indicators and troubleshoot issues. Some of the essential metrics include:

1. **Consumed Read Capacity Units:** This metric measures the read capacity units consumed by your table. High values may indicate inefficient queries or the need to adjust your provisioned capacity.
2. **Consumed Write Capacity Units:** Similar to the read capacity units metric, this one measures the write capacity units consumed by your table.
3. **Throttled Read Events:** Throttling occurs when your table's provisioned capacity is exceeded. This metric counts the number of times read requests are throttled.
4. **Throttled Write Events:** Like throttled read events, this metric counts the number of times write requests are throttled.
5. **Read and Write Latency:** These metrics track the time it takes for read and write operations to complete, helping you identify performance bottlenecks.
6. **Returned Item Count:** This metric shows the number of

items returned by queries and scans, allowing you to gauge the efficiency of your queries.

## Setting Up CloudWatch Alarms

To proactively monitor your DynamoDB tables, you can create CloudWatch alarms based on specific metrics. Alarms can notify you when a threshold is breached, enabling you to take immediate action. For example, you can set up alarms for:

- High levels of read or write capacity consumption
- Excessive throttling of read or write requests
- Elevated latency for read or write operations

When an alarm triggers, you can receive notifications via email, SMS, or other methods, allowing your team to respond promptly to performance issues.

## Log Analysis with CloudWatch Logs

In addition to metrics, CloudWatch Logs can capture log data from DynamoDB operations. By setting up log streams, you can analyze the details of each request, including the request parameters, response, and errors. This level of visibility is valuable for diagnosing issues, optimizing queries, and ensuring data integrity.

## Using CloudWatch Dashboards

CloudWatch allows you to create custom dashboards that display your DynamoDB metrics and logs in one place. Dashboards provide a centralized view of your resources' performance and can help you quickly identify trends and anomalies.

### Cost Considerations

Keep in mind that while CloudWatch provides valuable insights into your DynamoDB's performance, it also incurs costs based on the volume of data ingested and the number of alarms set up. Be mindful of your monitoring configuration to avoid unexpected charges.

In summary, Amazon CloudWatch is a powerful tool for monitoring and managing the performance of your DynamoDB resources. By leveraging CloudWatch metrics, alarms, logs, and dashboards, you can proactively detect and address performance issues, ensuring a smooth and efficient operation of your DynamoDB tables.

## 8.4 Caching Strategies with DAX

Amazon DynamoDB Accelerator (DAX) is a fully managed, highly available, and in-memory cache for DynamoDB. It can significantly improve the read performance of your DynamoDB tables by caching frequently accessed data and reducing the need to query the underlying tables. In this section, we'll explore the benefits of using DAX and how to implement caching strategies effectively.

### Why Use DAX?

#### *1. Faster Read Performance*

DAX caches frequently accessed items from DynamoDB tables in memory. When a read request is made, DAX can serve the data directly from the cache, resulting in much lower latencies compared to querying the DynamoDB table.

*2. Reduced DynamoDB Costs*

By offloading a significant portion of read traffic to DAX, you can potentially reduce the read capacity units (RCUs) and associated costs in your DynamoDB tables. This can lead to cost savings, especially for applications with high read workloads.

*3. Improved Scalability and Availability*

DAX is a fully managed service that automatically handles the provisioning and scaling of cache nodes. It also provides high availability by replicating data across multiple Availability Zones. This ensures that your cache remains responsive and reliable, even during failovers or maintenance events.

## Implementing Caching with DAX

To implement caching with DAX, you need to perform the following steps:

*1. Create a DAX Cluster*

Start by creating a DAX cluster in the AWS Management Console or using the AWS CLI. You specify the DynamoDB table(s) that you want to cache data from when creating the DAX cluster.

*2. Update Your Application*

Modify your application code to use the DAX client instead of the standard DynamoDB client. The DAX client provides the same APIs as the DynamoDB client but routes requests through the DAX cluster. This step is relatively straightforward, as the DAX client is compatible with existing code that uses the AWS SDK for DynamoDB.

*3. Configure the Cache*

DAX allows you to configure the cache behavior based on your application's requirements. You can set cache item time-to-live (TTL) values to control how long items remain in the cache. Additionally, you can define cache security groups to control access to the DAX cluster.

*4. Monitor and Optimize*

Once your application is using DAX, it's essential to monitor the cache's performance and usage. DAX provides CloudWatch metrics and logs that can help you gain insights into cache hits, misses, and overall performance. You can adjust the cache size and TTL settings based on your application's evolving needs.

## Considerations and Limitations

While DAX offers significant benefits, there are some considerations to keep in mind:

- DAX is primarily designed for read-heavy workloads. If your application has a predominantly write-heavy workload, DAX may not provide as much value.

- Cache consistency is crucial. DAX ensures strong consistency within the cache but does not provide cross-table consistency.

- There are additional costs associated with running a DAX cluster, so you should evaluate the cost-effectiveness based on your application's usage patterns.

In conclusion, Amazon DAX is a powerful tool for improving the read performance of your DynamoDB applications. By implementing caching strategies with DAX, you can reduce latency, lower DynamoDB costs, and enhance the overall scalability and availability of your applications. However, it's essential to carefully evaluate your application's requirements and workload characteristics before deciding to use DAX.

## 8.5 Fine-Tuning Indexes and Queries

Fine-tuning indexes and queries is a critical aspect of optimizing the performance of your Amazon DynamoDB tables. In this section, we'll delve into advanced techniques for optimizing your table's indexes and queries to achieve the best possible read and write performance.

### Utilizing Global Secondary Indexes (GSI)

#### *1. Choosing the Right Attributes*

When creating a Global Secondary Index (GSI), it's crucial to select the right attributes to include in the index key and projection. The choice of attributes impacts query performance and the size of the index. Consider the types of queries your application needs to support and include attributes that are frequently used in your query conditions.

*2. Sparse Indexes*

DynamoDB allows for sparse indexes, meaning that not all items in the table need to have the indexed attribute. This can be advantageous in scenarios where only a subset of items requires indexing. Sparse indexes can help reduce the size of the GSI and save on storage costs.

*3. Choosing Index Type*

DynamoDB offers two types of GSIs: projected and non-projected indexes. Projected indexes include all table attributes, while non-projected indexes only include specific attributes. Carefully choose between these types based on your query requirements and the amount of data you want to retrieve with each query.

## Query Optimization

*4. Query Filters vs. Post-Processing*

DynamoDB supports filtering results using query filters, but this is done after retrieving items from the index. If you need to filter a significant number of items, it's often more efficient to perform post-processing in your application code. This reduces the amount of data transferred from DynamoDB to your application.

*5. Efficient Use of Query and Scan*

DynamoDB offers two primary ways to retrieve data: Query and Scan. Query is more efficient as it retrieves items based on indexed attributes and is generally faster. Scan, on the other hand, examines all items in the table and should be used sparingly, mainly for operations that can't be achieved with a query.

## Batch Operations

### *6. Utilizing BatchGetItem and BatchWriteItem*

To optimize read and write operations, consider using BatchGetItem and BatchWriteItem operations. These allow you to retrieve or modify multiple items in a single request, reducing the number of round-trips to DynamoDB and improving efficiency.

### *7. Parallel Scans*

For large datasets that can't be efficiently queried or batched, you can perform parallel scans. Divide the table into segments and scan each segment concurrently, leveraging the parallel processing capabilities of your application.

## Monitoring and Fine-Tuning

### *8. Use CloudWatch Metrics*

Regularly monitor your DynamoDB table's performance using CloudWatch metrics. Look for trends in read and write capacity utilization, throttle events, and latency. Adjust provisioned capacity and indexes as needed to maintain optimal performance.

### *9. Adjust Provisioned Throughput*

DynamoDB allows you to provision read and write capacity for your table. Periodically review your application's traffic patterns and adjust provisioned capacity to ensure you're not under- or over-provisioned. DynamoDB auto-scaling can also help automate this process.

## Conclusion

Optimizing indexes and queries in Amazon DynamoDB can have a significant impact on your application's performance and cost-efficiency. By carefully selecting the right attributes for GSIs, optimizing queries, and utilizing batch operations, you can ensure that your DynamoDB tables deliver fast and reliable access to your data. Monitoring and fine-tuning are ongoing processes to maintain optimal performance as your application evolves.

# Chapter 9: Scalability and Reliability

## 9.1 DynamoDB's Distributed Architecture

Amazon DynamoDB is built on a distributed architecture that is designed for high availability, scalability, and fault tolerance. Understanding the core principles of DynamoDB's distributed system is essential for optimizing its performance and ensuring reliability.

### Data Partitioning

DynamoDB partitions data across multiple physical servers to ensure even distribution and efficient storage. Each partition is known as a "partition key range" and contains a range of items based on their partition key values. This distribution allows DynamoDB to handle large amounts of data and traffic by horizontally scaling across partitions.

### Partitions and Partition Keys

When you create a DynamoDB table, you define a primary key composed of one or two attributes: the partition key and an optional sort key. The partition key is used to determine which partition the item belongs to. It's crucial to choose a partition key that evenly distributes the workload across partitions to avoid "hot" partitions where a disproportionate amount of data is accessed.

### Data Distribution

DynamoDB automatically distributes data across partitions, and it's essential to understand how it does this. The distribution algorithm uses a hash function to map partition key values to specific partitions. This ensures that items with similar partition key values are stored in the same partition.

## Load Balancing

DynamoDB's distributed nature allows it to balance the workload efficiently. When a partition becomes too busy due to high read or write activity, DynamoDB automatically redistributes the partitions, ensuring that no partition is overloaded. This automatic load balancing is crucial for maintaining low-latency access to data.

## Data Replication

To ensure high availability and fault tolerance, DynamoDB replicates data across multiple Availability Zones within a region. This replication is done synchronously, meaning that writes are acknowledged only after the data is successfully replicated to multiple locations. In the event of a server or Availability Zone failure, DynamoDB can continue to serve data without interruption.

## Handling Failures

DynamoDB is designed to handle failures gracefully. When a server or network issue occurs, DynamoDB automatically detects it and redirects requests to healthy servers. This built-in fault tolerance minimizes downtime and ensures that your application can continue to access data even during failures.

## Conclusion

DynamoDB's distributed architecture is at the core of its scalability and reliability. Understanding how data partitioning, load balancing, data distribution, and replication work is essential for optimizing your DynamoDB tables. By leveraging the distributed nature of DynamoDB, you can build highly available and scalable applications that can handle a wide range of workloads.

## 9.2 Auto Scaling in DynamoDB

Auto Scaling in Amazon DynamoDB is a feature that automatically adjusts your table's provisioned read and write capacity in response to changes in traffic or workload. This ensures that your DynamoDB tables can handle varying levels of demand without manual intervention, reducing costs and simplifying capacity management.

### Understanding Auto Scaling Policies

When you enable Auto Scaling for a DynamoDB table, you define policies that specify the target utilization for your provisioned capacity. You can set policies for both read and write capacity separately. DynamoDB continuously monitors the consumed capacity and adjusts the provisioned capacity up or down to meet the specified utilization target.

### Creating Auto Scaling Policies

To create an Auto Scaling policy, you need to specify:

- The target utilization percentage (e.g., 70%)
- Minimum and maximum provisioned capacity values
- The scaling adjustment type (either "ChangeInCapacity" or "PercentChangeInCapacity")
- The scaling adjustment value (how much to increase or decrease capacity)

Here's an example of creating an Auto Scaling policy using the AWS Command Line Interface (CLI):

aws application-autoscaling put-scaling-policy \

—service-namespace dynamodb \

—resource-id "table/<Your-TableName>" \

—scalable-dimension "dynamodb:table:ReadCapacityUnits" \

—policy-name "MyReadAutoScalingPolicy" \

—policy-type "TargetTrackingScaling" \

—target-tracking-scaling-policy-configuration file://read-auto-scaling-config.json

## Monitoring and Alarms

DynamoDB provides CloudWatch metrics that allow you to monitor the performance and capacity utilization of your tables. You can set up CloudWatch alarms based on these metrics to trigger Auto Scaling actions when certain conditions are met. For example, you can create an alarm to scale up your read capacity when the consumed capacity exceeds a certain threshold for a specified duration.

## Automatic Scaling

Once you've configured Auto Scaling policies and alarms, DynamoDB takes care of the rest. It automatically adjusts the provisioned capacity up or down in response to changes in workload. This means that during traffic spikes, DynamoDB can increase capacity to handle the load, and during periods of low activity, it can reduce capacity to save costs.

## Cost Optimization

Auto Scaling helps optimize costs by ensuring that you don't overprovision capacity when it's not needed. You pay only for the capacity you actually use, which can result in significant cost savings compared to manually managing provisioned capacity.

## Best Practices

When using Auto Scaling in DynamoDB, consider the following best practices:

- Define meaningful CloudWatch alarms based on your workload patterns.
- Use a combination of target tracking and step scaling policies for fine-grained control.
- Regularly monitor and adjust your Auto Scaling configurations to align with changing workload patterns.
- Understand the billing implications of Auto Scaling and ensure that it fits your cost optimization goals.

In conclusion, Auto Scaling in DynamoDB is a powerful feature that allows you to automatically adjust capacity based on your application's needs. By configuring Auto Scaling policies and alarms effectively, you can ensure that your DynamoDB tables are cost-efficient and able to handle varying workloads with ease.

# 9.3 Handling Spikes and Load Balancing

In Amazon DynamoDB, handling spikes in traffic and load balancing is a critical aspect of maintaining the performance and reliability of your applications. Spikes in traffic can occur unexpectedly due to various reasons, such as marketing campaigns, promotions, or sudden increases in user activity. To ensure that your DynamoDB tables can handle these spikes without experiencing performance degradation, you need to implement effective strategies for handling increased load.

## Provisioned Capacity

One way to handle spikes in traffic is by provisioning sufficient read and write capacity in advance. DynamoDB offers two modes for provisioning capacity: On-Demand and Provisioned. In the Provisioned mode, you specify the read and write capacity units for your table, and DynamoDB allocates those resources to you. By carefully monitoring your application's usage patterns and setting appropriate provisioned capacity levels, you can ensure that your table can handle anticipated spikes.

## Auto Scaling

While provisioned capacity is effective for handling predictable spikes, it may not be suitable for handling sudden, unexpected surges in traffic. This is where Auto Scaling, as discussed in the previous section (9.2), comes into play. Auto Scaling automatically adjusts your table's provisioned capacity in response to changes in traffic, allowing your table to handle both expected and unexpected spikes.

## Using Provisioned Capacity and Auto Scaling Together

A common strategy is to combine provisioned capacity and Auto Scaling. You can provision a baseline capacity that covers your normal workload and configure Auto Scaling policies to handle unexpected spikes. For example, you might provision 100 read capacity units and configure an Auto Scaling policy to increase capacity by 50% when the consumed capacity exceeds 70%.

## Load Balancing

Load balancing can further enhance your DynamoDB application's ability to handle spikes. By distributing the read and write requests across multiple partitions and replicas, you can achieve better scalability and fault tolerance. DynamoDB handles load balancing behind the scenes, ensuring that requests are evenly distributed.

## Optimizing Queries

Another aspect of handling spikes is optimizing your queries. Inefficient queries can place additional load on your DynamoDB tables. Utilize DynamoDB's efficient querying techniques, such as using secondary indexes and specifying appropriate query conditions, to reduce the impact of spikes on your tables.

## Caching

Consider implementing caching mechanisms to reduce the load on DynamoDB during spikes. Services like Amazon ElastiCache can be used to cache frequently accessed data, reducing the number of queries hitting your DynamoDB tables.

## Monitoring and Alarms

Regularly monitor the performance of your DynamoDB tables using CloudWatch metrics and set up alarms to notify you of any unusual activity or performance degradation. This proactive monitoring approach allows you to address issues before they impact your application's users.

In conclusion, handling spikes and load balancing in Amazon DynamoDB is essential for ensuring the reliability and performance of your applications. By combining provisioned capacity, Auto Scaling, load balancing, query optimization, caching, and effective monitoring, you can build applications that gracefully handle fluctuations in traffic and deliver a seamless user experience.

## 9.4 Backup and Restore Strategies

Ensuring data resilience and availability is a critical aspect of managing Amazon DynamoDB tables. DynamoDB provides built-in features for creating backups and restoring data, allowing you to recover from accidental data loss, corruption, or system failures.

### On-Demand Backups

DynamoDB offers on-demand backups, which allow you to create full backups of your tables at any time. These backups capture the entire table, including its schema and data. You can create backups manually or programmatically using the AWS Management Console, AWS CLI, or SDKs.

To create an on-demand backup, you specify the table you want to back up, and DynamoDB handles the rest. You can also set a point-in-time recovery (PITR) attribute, which enables you to restore the table to any point in time within a specified retention period.

```
import boto3

# Create a DynamoDB client

dynamodb = boto3.client('dynamodb')
```

```
# Specify the table name
table_name = 'YourTableName'
# Create an on-demand backup
response = dynamodb.create_backup(
TableName=table_name,
BackupName='MyBackup',
)
# Enable point-in-time recovery for the table
dynamodb.update_continuous_backups(
TableName=table_name,
PointInTimeRecoverySpecification={
'PointInTimeRecoveryEnabled': True
}
)
```

## Automated Backups

DynamoDB also provides automated backups, which are enabled by default when you create a new table. These backups are taken daily and retained for a specified duration, typically 35 days. Automated backups are an excellent option for safeguarding your data without manual intervention.

## Restoring from Backups

To restore a table from a backup, you can use the AWS Management Console, AWS CLI, or SDKs. When restoring, you can choose to create a new table or overwrite an existing one with the same name.

```
# Restore a table from a backup

response = dynamodb.restore_table_to_point_in_time(

SourceTableName=table_name,

TargetTableName='RestoredTable',

UseLatestRestorableTime=True

)
```

## Best Practices for Backup and Restore

1. **Regularly Create Backups**: Establish a backup strategy that includes both on-demand and automated backups. Regularly create on-demand backups before making significant changes to your data.
2. **Enable Point-in-Time Recovery (PITR)**: Enable PITR for critical tables to have the ability to restore data to any point within the retention period.
3. **Test Restores**: Periodically perform test restores to ensure that your backup and restore processes are functioning as expected.
4. **Monitor Backup Costs**: Be aware of the storage costs associated with backups, especially if you have a high volume of data. Adjust your retention period accordingly.
5. **Document Restore Procedures**: Document the steps required to restore a table from a backup, including any

specific configurations or settings.

6. **Consider Cross-Region Replication**: For mission-critical applications, consider setting up cross-region replication to further protect your data in case of regional outages.

In summary, backup and restore strategies are crucial for maintaining data availability and reliability in Amazon DynamoDB. By leveraging on-demand and automated backups, enabling point-in-time recovery, and following best practices, you can safeguard your data and minimize downtime in the event of data loss or corruption.

## 9.5 Ensuring High Availability and Disaster Recovery

High availability and disaster recovery (HA/DR) are critical considerations when designing and operating Amazon DynamoDB tables. HA/DR strategies are essential for ensuring that your applications remain accessible and resilient in the face of unforeseen incidents or infrastructure failures. In this section, we'll explore best practices and features to achieve high availability and disaster recovery in DynamoDB.

### Multi-Region Replication

One of the most effective ways to achieve high availability and disaster recovery in DynamoDB is by implementing multi-region replication. DynamoDB Global Tables allow you to replicate your data across multiple AWS regions, ensuring that your application can continue to operate even if an entire region becomes unavailable.

To create a Global Table, you select the primary region where you create and manage the table and then specify one or more replica regions where copies of the table data will be stored. DynamoDB takes care of replicating data asynchronously across these regions, ensuring low-latency access to data.

```
import boto3

# Create a DynamoDB client

dynamodb = boto3.client('dynamodb')

# Specify the table name

table_name = 'YourTableName'

# Create a Global Table with replica regions

response = dynamodb.create_global_table(

TableName=table_name,

ReplicationGroup=[

{

'RegionName': 'us-west-2' # Replica region

},

{

'RegionName': 'eu-west-1' # Another replica region

}

]

)
```

## Failover and Read/Write Routing

With a Global Table, you can configure automatic failover and read/write routing policies. In the event of a regional outage, DynamoDB automatically promotes a replica to become the new primary table, ensuring continuous availability.

```
# Configure automatic failover for a Global Table

dynamodb.update_global_table(

TableName=table_name,

GlobalTableName='YourGlobalTableName',

ReplicaUpdates=[

{

'Create': {

'RegionName': 'us-east-1' # New primary region in case of failover

}

},

{

'Delete': {

'RegionName': 'us-west-2' # Region to be removed from Global Table

}

}

]
```

)

## Point-in-Time Recovery (PITR)

Enabling Point-in-Time Recovery (PITR) for your DynamoDB table is essential for disaster recovery. PITR allows you to restore your table to any point in time within a specified retention period, which can be a lifesaver in cases of accidental data deletion or corruption.

## Monitoring and Alarming

Implement comprehensive monitoring and alarming for your DynamoDB tables. AWS CloudWatch and AWS CloudTrail can help you track performance metrics, detect anomalies, and troubleshoot issues. Set up alarms to receive notifications when specific thresholds are breached, allowing you to respond proactively to potential problems.

## Regular Testing and Drills

Perform regular failover testing and disaster recovery drills to validate your HA/DR setup. These tests should simulate real-world scenarios and help you identify any gaps in your recovery procedures.

## Data Archiving and Offsite Backups

Consider implementing data archiving and offsite backups as part of your disaster recovery plan. Storing backups in a different AWS region or on a separate cloud provider can provide an additional layer of protection against regional outages or data center failures.

## Summary

High availability and disaster recovery are crucial for maintaining business continuity and data resilience in Amazon DynamoDB. By leveraging multi-region replication, failover mechanisms, PITR, monitoring, testing, and offsite backups, you can ensure that your DynamoDB-powered applications remain highly available and recoverable in the face of unexpected challenges and disasters.

# 10.1 Access Control and IAM Roles

Access control is a fundamental aspect of securing your Amazon DynamoDB resources and ensuring that only authorized users and applications can interact with your data. In this section, we will explore how to set up access control using AWS Identity and Access Management (IAM) roles and policies to enforce fine-grained permissions for DynamoDB operations.

## AWS Identity and Access Management (IAM)

AWS Identity and Access Management (IAM) is a service that allows you to manage access to your AWS resources. IAM enables you to create and manage IAM users, groups, and roles, and assign permissions to them. To control access to DynamoDB, you can create IAM roles with specific policies that define what actions can be performed on DynamoDB tables.

Here's an example of how to create an IAM role for DynamoDB access:

```
{
"Version": "2012-10-17",
"Statement": [
{
"Effect": "Allow",
"Action": [
"dynamodb:DescribeTable",
```

"dynamodb:GetItem",

"dynamodb:PutItem",

"dynamodb:UpdateItem",

"dynamodb:DeleteItem"

],

"Resource": "arn:aws:dynamodb:us-east-1:123456789012:table/YourTableName"

}

]

}

In the policy above, we specify that the role is allowed to perform actions like GetItem, PutItem, UpdateItem, and DeleteItem on a specific DynamoDB table identified by its Amazon Resource Name (ARN).

## IAM Roles for Applications

When you develop applications that interact with DynamoDB, it's a best practice to use IAM roles for granting permissions. Instead of hardcoding access credentials in your application code, you can assign an IAM role to an AWS resource like an EC2 instance, Lambda function, or ECS task.

Your application code can then automatically assume the IAM role when making requests to DynamoDB, ensuring secure and auditable access. Here's an example of how to assume an IAM role in Python using the AWS SDK:

```
import boto3

# Create an STS client

sts_client = boto3.client('sts')

# Assume the IAM role

response = sts_client.assume_role(

RoleArn='arn:aws:iam::123456789012:role/
YourDynamoDBRole',

RoleSessionName='DynamoDBSession'

)

# Use the temporary credentials

dynamodb = boto3.client('dynamodb',

aws_access_key_id=response['Credentials']['AccessKeyId'],

aws_secret_access_key=response['Credentials']['SecretAccessKey'],

aws_session_token=response['Credentials']['SessionToken']

)

# Now, you can use DynamoDB with the assumed role's permissions

response = dynamodb.put_item(...)
```

## Fine-Grained Access Control

IAM policies can be fine-tuned to provide granular access control. You can specify conditions, such as restricting access based on IP address, requiring MFA (Multi-Factor Authentication), or limiting access to specific actions within DynamoDB tables.

IAM also supports policy variables that allow you to dynamically control access based on attributes like the requester's IP address, the current time, or even the requested resource's name.

```
{
"Version": "2012-10-17",
"Statement": [
{
"Effect": "Allow",
"Action": "dynamodb:Query",
"Resource": "arn:aws:dynamodb:us-east-1:123456789012:table/YourTableName",
"Condition": {
"IpAddress": {
"aws:SourceIp": "192.168.1.0/24"
}
}
}
]
}
```

This policy grants Query access to the DynamoDB table only if the request originates from the specified IP address range.

## IAM Best Practices

Here are some IAM best practices for securing DynamoDB:

1. **Least Privilege**: Assign the minimum required permissions to IAM roles and users to limit exposure.
2. **Rotate Credentials**: Regularly rotate access keys and IAM role sessions to enhance security.
3. **Use Managed Policies**: Prefer AWS managed policies or customer-managed policies over inline policies for better maintainability.
4. **Audit and Monitor**: Enable AWS CloudTrail to log IAM actions and set up CloudWatch alarms for suspicious activities.
5. **Test Permissions**: Use IAM policy simulator to test and validate permissions before deploying them.
6. **IAM Conditions**: Leverage conditions in IAM policies to control access based on various factors.

By following these practices, you can establish robust access control mechanisms for your DynamoDB tables, safeguard your data, and maintain compliance with security standards and regulations.

## 10.2 Data Encryption at Rest and in Transit

Securing data is paramount in any database system, and Amazon DynamoDB offers robust encryption options to protect your data both at rest and in transit. In this section, we'll explore how to ensure the confidentiality and integrity of your data through encryption mechanisms.

## Data Encryption at Rest

### *Server-Side Encryption (SSE)*

DynamoDB provides Server-Side Encryption (SSE) to automatically encrypt your data at rest. When you create a DynamoDB table, you can enable SSE, and DynamoDB takes care of the encryption process transparently. SSE supports two modes:

1. **SSE with AWS-Managed Keys (SSE-S3)**: In this mode, DynamoDB uses AWS-managed keys to encrypt your data. You don't need to manage encryption keys yourself, making it a hassle-free option.
2. **SSE with Customer-Managed Keys (SSE-C)**: If you require more control over your encryption keys, you can use SSE-C. With SSE-C, you provide your own encryption keys, and DynamoDB uses them to encrypt and decrypt data.

Enabling SSE is as simple as selecting the encryption option when creating your DynamoDB table:

```
"ProvisionedThroughput": {
"ReadCapacityUnits": 5,
"WriteCapacityUnits": 5
},
"SSESpecification": {
"Enabled": true,
"SSEType": "AES256"
```

```
}
```

### *Data Key Encryption*

Under SSE-C, DynamoDB uses a data key to encrypt and decrypt your data. The data key itself is encrypted using a master key managed by AWS Key Management Service (KMS) or your own master key. This multi-layered encryption adds an extra level of security to your data.

## Data Encryption in Transit

### *HTTPS Endpoints*

To protect data in transit, DynamoDB offers HTTPS endpoints for all API calls. This ensures that data transmitted between your application and DynamoDB is encrypted using secure TLS/SSL protocols. You don't need to configure anything extra for this encryption; it's built into the service.

## Best Practices

When working with data encryption in DynamoDB, consider the following best practices:

1. **Use SSE**: Enable Server-Side Encryption for your DynamoDB tables, choosing the appropriate mode based on your requirements.
2. **Key Management**: If using SSE-C, carefully manage your encryption keys, and consider using AWS KMS for added security and control.
3. **HTTPS**: Always use HTTPS when interacting with DynamoDB through API calls to ensure data in transit is

encrypted.

4. **Audit and Monitor**: Regularly audit your encryption configurations and monitor for any anomalies or security events using AWS services like CloudTrail and CloudWatch.
5. **Security Protocols**: Stay informed about security best practices and updates from AWS, and keep your DynamoDB encryption mechanisms up to date.

By following these practices, you can ensure that your data remains secure and compliant with industry standards and regulations while using Amazon DynamoDB.

## 10.3 Auditing with AWS CloudTrail

Auditing and monitoring are essential components of a robust security strategy when working with Amazon DynamoDB. AWS CloudTrail is a service that provides detailed logs of all AWS API calls made in your AWS account, including those made to DynamoDB. In this section, we'll explore how to set up and use AWS CloudTrail for auditing your DynamoDB activity.

### Enabling AWS CloudTrail

To get started with AWS CloudTrail for DynamoDB, follow these steps:

1. **Sign in to AWS Console**: Log in to your AWS Management Console using your AWS account credentials.
2. **Open CloudTrail**: Navigate to the AWS CloudTrail service from the AWS Management Console.
3. **Create a New Trail**: Click on the "Trails" in the

CloudTrail dashboard and then click "Create Trail."

4. **Configure Trail Settings**:

– **Trail Name**: Give your trail a descriptive name.

– **Storage Location**: Choose an S3 bucket where CloudTrail will store logs.

– **Apply trail to all regions**: Enable this option if you want to capture data from all AWS regions.

1. **Select DynamoDB as a Data Event Source**: Under "Data events," click "Add data event." In the "Event Source" dropdown, select "DynamoDB" to enable data event logging for DynamoDB.
2. **Specify Read and Write Events**: You can configure the specific read and write events you want to monitor for DynamoDB. For example, you can choose to log all read and write operations or only specific ones, such as "GetItem" or "PutItem."
3. **Create or Choose an Existing S3 Bucket**: CloudTrail logs are stored in an S3 bucket. You can create a new bucket or choose an existing one.
4. **Review and Create**: Review your trail settings and create the trail.

## Accessing DynamoDB Audit Logs

Once CloudTrail is configured, it will start capturing API events related to your DynamoDB resources. These logs are invaluable for auditing and security analysis. You can access the logs in the following ways:

*AWS Management Console*

1. **Navigate to CloudTrail**: Go to the AWS CloudTrail console.
2. **Select Your Trail**: Choose the trail you created for DynamoDB.
3. **View Events**: You can view events directly from the console. Filter and search for specific DynamoDB-related events to audit activity.

*AWS CLI*

You can also use the AWS Command Line Interface (CLI) to query and analyze CloudTrail logs programmatically.

*# List CloudTrail events related to DynamoDB*

aws cloudtrail lookup-events—lookup-attributes AttributeKey=EventSource,AttributeValue=dynamodb.amazonaws.com

*Amazon S3*

CloudTrail logs are stored in an S3 bucket, which you specified during setup. You can access logs directly from the S3 bucket using the S3 console or programmatically.

## Monitoring and Alerts

To enhance security, consider setting up alerts and notifications based on specific DynamoDB events or patterns in CloudTrail logs. AWS CloudWatch can be used to create custom alarms that trigger notifications when certain conditions are met.

In conclusion, AWS CloudTrail is a powerful tool for auditing and monitoring DynamoDB activity. By setting up CloudTrail and analyzing its logs, you can gain valuable insights into who is accessing your DynamoDB resources, what actions are being performed, and detect any suspicious or unauthorized activity, helping you maintain a secure and compliant environment.

## 10.4 Compliance and Data Protection

Ensuring compliance with various regulatory requirements and protecting sensitive data are critical aspects of managing Amazon DynamoDB. In this section, we'll explore compliance considerations and data protection measures when working with DynamoDB.

### Compliance Requirements

#### *GDPR (General Data Protection Regulation)*

If your DynamoDB application involves processing personal data of European Union (EU) citizens, you must comply with the GDPR. Some key considerations include:

- **Data Minimization**: Collect and store only the data necessary for your application.
- **Data Subject Rights**: Implement mechanisms to handle data subject requests for access, rectification, and erasure.
- **Consent**: Obtain explicit consent for data processing when required.
- **Data Portability**: Enable users to request their data in a structured, machine-readable format.

*HIPAA (Health Insurance Portability and Accountability Act)*

For healthcare applications, DynamoDB should adhere to HIPAA regulations, which involve safeguards for protected health information (PHI). Key requirements include:

- **Data Encryption**: Implement encryption at rest and in transit for PHI.
- **Audit Trails**: Maintain detailed audit logs of PHI access and changes.
- **Access Control**: Ensure that only authorized personnel can access PHI.
- **Business Associate Agreements (BAAs)**: Sign BAAs with AWS to formalize HIPAA compliance.

*CCPA (California Consumer Privacy Act)*

For businesses handling the personal information of California residents, CCPA compliance is essential. Key aspects include:

- **Data Mapping**: Understand and document the flow of personal data within your application.
- **Data Access Rights**: Allow users to request their data and opt-out of data sales.
- **Data Security**: Implement reasonable security measures to protect personal information.

*PCI DSS (Payment Card Industry Data Security Standard)*

If your application deals with credit card data, PCI DSS compliance is mandatory. Key requirements include:

- **Data Encryption**: Securely store and transmit cardholder data using encryption.
- **Access Control**: Restrict access to cardholder data to authorized personnel only.
- **Regular Security Testing**: Conduct regular vulnerability assessments and penetration testing.

## Data Protection Measures

### *Encryption*

- **At Rest**: Enable encryption at rest for DynamoDB tables using AWS Key Management Service (KMS) keys.
- **In Transit**: Use SSL/TLS to encrypt data in transit between your application and DynamoDB.

### *Access Control*

- **AWS Identity and Access Management (IAM)**: Define fine-grained access policies for DynamoDB resources.
- **Attribute-Based Access Control (ABAC)**: Implement ABAC to control access based on attribute values.

*Auditing and Logging*

- **AWS CloudTrail**: Enable CloudTrail to capture API activity related to DynamoDB, facilitating auditing and monitoring.
- **Amazon CloudWatch Logs**: Stream DynamoDB event logs to CloudWatch Logs for real-time monitoring.

*Data Masking and Redaction*

- Implement data masking or redaction techniques to protect sensitive information in query results and logs.

*Regular Audits and Assessments*

- Conduct regular security audits, vulnerability assessments, and penetration testing to identify and remediate security weaknesses.

*Incident Response Plan*

- Develop and maintain an incident response plan to address security incidents promptly and effectively.

By following these compliance considerations and data protection measures, you can ensure that your DynamoDB application complies with relevant regulations and safeguards sensitive data, fostering trust among users and stakeholders.

## 10.5 Best Practices for Secure Data Management

In this section, we will explore best practices for secure data management in Amazon DynamoDB. Ensuring the security of your data is of paramount importance, and DynamoDB provides several features and best practices to help you achieve this goal.

### 1. Use AWS Identity and Access Management (IAM)

**IAM** is a fundamental service in AWS that controls access to various AWS resources, including DynamoDB. Follow these IAM best practices:

- **Least Privilege**: Grant users and services the minimum permissions required to perform their tasks.

- **Role-Based Access**: Use IAM roles for EC2 instances, Lambda functions, and other AWS resources to access DynamoDB securely.

- **Multi-Factor Authentication (MFA)**: Enable MFA for your AWS accounts to add an extra layer of security.

### 2. Enable Encryption

Encrypting your data both at rest and in transit is crucial for data security:

- **Encryption at Rest**: Enable DynamoDB's encryption at rest feature, which uses AWS Key Management Service (KMS) for key management.

- **Encryption in Transit**: Ensure that all communication between your application and DynamoDB is encrypted using SSL/TLS.

## 3. Implement Fine-Grained Access Control

To control access to your DynamoDB tables and data at a granular level, consider these best practices:

- **Attribute-Based Access Control (ABAC)**: Use ABAC to restrict access to specific attributes within an item based on attribute values.

- **Conditional Expressions**: Utilize DynamoDB's conditional expressions to enforce data access conditions.

## 4. Monitor and Audit Activity

Maintaining visibility into your DynamoDB environment is vital for security:

- **AWS CloudTrail**: Enable CloudTrail to log all API activity related to DynamoDB, allowing you to track changes and access attempts.

- **Amazon CloudWatch**: Use CloudWatch to set up alarms for unusual activity and to monitor performance metrics.

## 5. Regularly Backup Data

Implement a backup strategy to protect your data from accidental deletions or corruptions:

- **DynamoDB Continuous Backups**: Enable continuous backups to create automatic backups of your data, stored for 35 days.

- **Point-in-Time Recovery (PITR)**: Enable PITR to recover your data to any second in the backup retention period.

## 6. Secure Your Applications

Ensure that your applications accessing DynamoDB follow secure coding practices:

- **Parameterization**: Use parameterized queries to prevent injection attacks like SQL injection.

- **Authentication**: Implement strong authentication mechanisms for your application users.

- **Data Validation**: Sanitize and validate user input to prevent common security vulnerabilities.

## 7. Regularly Update and Patch

Keep your AWS resources, including DynamoDB, up to date with the latest security patches and updates. AWS regularly releases patches to address security vulnerabilities.

## 8. Disaster Recovery Planning

Plan for disaster recovery by creating and testing a recovery plan for your DynamoDB tables and data. Consider using AWS services like Global Tables for cross-region replication.

## 9. Educate Your Team

Security is a shared responsibility. Educate your team about security best practices and conduct regular security training sessions.

## 10. Perform Security Audits

Regularly perform security audits, vulnerability assessments, and penetration testing to identify and address security weaknesses in your DynamoDB setup.

By following these best practices, you can enhance the security of your Amazon DynamoDB environment and protect your data from various threats and vulnerabilities. Security should be an ongoing concern, and staying informed about emerging threats is essential for maintaining a secure DynamoDB deployment.

---

Chapter 11: Advanced Features and Services 11.1 DynamoDB Streams for Real-time Processing

---

# Chapter 11: Advanced Features and Services

## Section 11.1: DynamoDB Streams for Real-time Processing

DynamoDB Streams is a powerful feature that enables real-time data processing and analysis of changes made to your DynamoDB tables. It provides a chronological log of item-level modifications, such as inserts, updates, and deletes, and makes these changes available to downstream applications and services for further processing. In this section, we will explore the capabilities of DynamoDB Streams and how you can leverage it in various scenarios.

### Understanding DynamoDB Streams

DynamoDB Streams is essentially a time-ordered sequence of item-level changes that occur in a DynamoDB table. These changes are captured and stored in a stream, allowing you to access historical and real-time data updates. Each stream record represents a single modification to an item in the table.

One of the key benefits of DynamoDB Streams is its ability to provide near-real-time data updates to applications. When an item in a table is modified, a corresponding record is immediately added to the stream. This can be useful for scenarios where you need to react to changes in your data in real-time, such as updating search indexes or triggering notifications.

### Enabling DynamoDB Streams

To use DynamoDB Streams, you need to enable it on a DynamoDB table. When you enable Streams for a table, DynamoDB automatically creates a stream associated with that table. You can choose between two stream view types: NEW_IMAGE and OLD_IMAGE.

- NEW_IMAGE: This view type includes the new version of the modified item after the change has occurred.
- OLD_IMAGE: This view type includes the old version of the modified item before the change has occurred.

You can select the appropriate view type based on your application's needs. For example, if you want to track changes made to an item, you can choose NEW_IMAGE to access the updated item.

## Consuming DynamoDB Streams

Once you have enabled DynamoDB Streams on a table, you can start consuming the stream data using various AWS services and SDKs. The most common way to consume stream data is by using AWS Lambda, a serverless compute service that can process and react to changes in the stream.

Here's a high-level overview of how you can use AWS Lambda with DynamoDB Streams:

1. Create a Lambda function: Write a Lambda function that defines the logic you want to execute in response to stream events.
2. Configure the trigger: Associate the Lambda function with the DynamoDB table's stream. This tells Lambda to invoke the function whenever there are new stream records.
3. Process the stream records: In your Lambda function, you can access the stream records and perform actions based on

the changes, such as updating other services, sending notifications, or storing data in another database.

### Use Cases for DynamoDB Streams

DynamoDB Streams can be used in various scenarios, including:

- Real-time analytics: Analyze changes in your data as they happen to gain insights and make data-driven decisions.

- Data synchronization: Keep multiple data sources in sync by replicating changes across systems.

- Notifications and triggers: Send notifications or trigger events based on specific changes to your data.

- Audit trails and compliance: Maintain a comprehensive record of all changes made to your data for auditing and compliance purposes.

In conclusion, DynamoDB Streams is a valuable feature that adds real-time capabilities to DynamoDB, making it suitable for a wider range of applications. By capturing and processing item-level changes, you can build real-time data pipelines and enable reactive applications that respond to changes in your data in near-real-time. This feature enhances DynamoDB's versatility and opens up new possibilities for building scalable and responsive applications.

## Section 11.2: Integrating with Lambda for Serverless Architectures

Integrating DynamoDB Streams with AWS Lambda is a powerful way to build serverless architectures that respond to changes in your data in real-time. In this section, we will explore how you can set up this integration, allowing you to create responsive and scalable applications without managing servers.

## Setting Up the Integration

To integrate DynamoDB Streams with AWS Lambda, follow these steps:

1. **Create a Lambda Function:** Start by creating a Lambda function that will process the DynamoDB stream events. You can define this function using the AWS Lambda Management Console or by using infrastructure-as-code tools like AWS CloudFormation or the Serverless Framework.
2. **Configure the Trigger:** In the Lambda function configuration, add a trigger that connects it to the DynamoDB table's stream. You can specify the batch size, which determines how many stream records are processed in each Lambda invocation. AWS Lambda will automatically invoke the function whenever new stream records are available.
3. **Handle Stream Events:** In your Lambda function code, you will need to implement logic to handle the stream events. The event payload contains information about the changes made to items in the DynamoDB table, allowing you to react to inserts, updates, and deletes.

## Sample Lambda Function

Here's a simplified example of a Lambda function that processes DynamoDB stream events:

```
import json
```

```
def lambda_handler(event, context):

for record in event['Records']:

# Parse the DynamoDB stream record

if record['eventName'] == 'INSERT':

# Handle insert event

new_image = record['dynamodb']['NewImage']

# Process the new item data

print(f"New item added: {json.dumps(new_image)}")

elif record['eventName'] == 'MODIFY':

# Handle update event

old_image = record['dynamodb']['OldImage']

new_image = record['dynamodb']['NewImage']

# Compare and process changes

print(f"Item modified - Old: {json.dumps(old_image)}, New: {json.dumps(new_image)}")

elif record['eventName'] == 'REMOVE':

# Handle delete event

old_image = record['dynamodb']['OldImage']

# Process deleted item data

print(f"Item deleted: {json.dumps(old_image)}")
```

In this example, the Lambda function processes insert, update, and delete events from the DynamoDB stream and prints information about the changes. In a real-world scenario, you can perform more advanced operations, such as updating other services, sending notifications, or storing data in another database.

## Benefits of Serverless Integration

Integrating DynamoDB Streams with AWS Lambda offers several advantages:

1. **Scalability:** Serverless functions automatically scale with the volume of stream events, ensuring that your application can handle changes in load without manual intervention.
2. **Cost-Efficiency:** You pay only for the compute resources used during function invocations, making it cost-effective, especially for applications with variable workloads.
3. **Real-Time Responsiveness:** Your application can respond to changes in data as they happen, providing a real-time user experience and reducing latency.
4. **Simplified Management:** Serverless architectures abstract infrastructure management, allowing you to focus on application logic rather than server provisioning and maintenance.
5. **Fault Tolerance:** AWS Lambda automatically manages fault tolerance, ensuring that your functions are highly available and can handle errors gracefully.

By leveraging the serverless capabilities of AWS Lambda and the real-time data processing provided by DynamoDB Streams, you can build responsive and scalable applications that meet the demands of modern, data-driven use cases. This integration is particularly valuable for applications that require near-real-time processing of data changes without the need to manage servers.

---

# Section 11.3: Data Export and Import Techniques

In this section, we will explore techniques for exporting and importing data in Amazon DynamoDB. DynamoDB provides several tools and methods to facilitate data migration, backup, and restore operations, making it versatile for various data management scenarios.

## 1. Exporting Data from DynamoDB

### *1.1. Using Data Pipeline*

Amazon Data Pipeline is a service that enables you to export data from DynamoDB to various destinations, such as Amazon S3, Amazon Redshift, or other AWS services. It allows you to schedule and automate data export tasks, making it suitable for regular backups or data warehousing.

To export data from DynamoDB using Data Pipeline:

1. Create a Data Pipeline in the AWS Management Console.
2. Configure the pipeline's data source as DynamoDB.
3. Specify the destination, such as an S3 bucket, and define the data format (e.g., JSON, CSV).
4. Set up the schedule for the export operation.

### *1.2. Using the AWS SDK*

You can also export data from DynamoDB programmatically using the AWS SDKs. This method gives you fine-grained control over the export process and allows you to integrate data exports into your application logic.

Here's a simplified example in Python using the AWS SDK (Boto3) to export data to an S3 bucket:

```
import boto3

# Initialize DynamoDB and S3 clients

dynamodb = boto3.client('dynamodb')

s3 = boto3.client('s3')

# Define the export parameters

export_params = {

'TableArn': 'arn:aws:dynamodb:us-east-1:123456789012:table/MyTable',

'S3Bucket': 'my-export-bucket',

'S3Prefix': 'exports/',

'ExportFormat': 'DYNAMODB_JSON'

}

# Start the export job

response = dynamodb.export_table_to_point_in_time(**export_params)
```

```
# Monitor the export job status and progress

while response['ExportDescription']['ExportStatus'] != 'COMPLETED':

response = dynamodb.describe_export(**export_params)

print(f"Export Status: {response['ExportDescription']['ExportStatus']}")
```

## 2. Importing Data into DynamoDB

### *2.1. Using the AWS SDK*

To import data into DynamoDB, you can use the AWS SDKs and the BatchWriteItem operation, which allows you to write multiple items to a table in a single request. You can prepare your data in JSON or CSV format and use SDK functions to batch-write items.

Here's an example of importing data into DynamoDB using Python and the AWS SDK (Boto3):

```
import boto3

# Initialize DynamoDB client

dynamodb = boto3.client('dynamodb')

# Define the batch write request

batch_write_request = [

{

'PutRequest': {

'Item': {
```

```
'CustomerId': {'N': '123'},
'Name': {'S': 'John Doe'},
'Email': {'S': 'john.doe@example.com'}
}
}
},
{
'PutRequest': {
'Item': {
'CustomerId': {'N': '456'},
'Name': {'S': 'Jane Smith'},
'Email': {'S': 'jane.smith@example.com'}
}
}
}
]
# Specify the target table
table_name = 'MyTable'
# Perform the batch write operation
```

response = dynamodb.batch_write_item(RequestItems={table_name: batch_write_request})

*# Check the response for any unprocessed items*

**if** response.get('UnprocessedItems'):

print("Some items were not processed.")

## 3. Data Export and Import Considerations

When working with data export and import in DynamoDB, consider the following:

- **Data Formats:** DynamoDB supports various data formats, including JSON, CSV, and others, depending on your use case.
- **Data Volume:** For large datasets, use data pipeline services or parallel processing to ensure efficient export and import.
- **Provisioned Throughput:** Be mindful of your table's provisioned throughput when performing batch writes or reads during imports.

These data export and import techniques enable you to manage your data efficiently in DynamoDB, whether it's for backup, migration, or integration with other AWS services. Choose the method that best suits your requirements and application architecture.

# Section 11.4: Working with Global Tables

In this section, we will delve into the concept of Global Tables in Amazon DynamoDB. Global Tables provide a powerful mechanism for creating highly available and globally distributed DynamoDB databases that can serve read and write requests with low latency across multiple AWS regions.

## 1. Understanding Global Tables

A Global Table is a multi-region, multi-master database in DynamoDB. It allows you to replicate your DynamoDB table data across multiple AWS regions, ensuring high availability and fault tolerance. Global Tables consist of one primary region and one or more replica regions.

Key points about Global Tables:

- **Primary Region:** The primary region is where you perform all write operations (creates, updates, deletes). DynamoDB automatically replicates these changes to the replica regions.

- **Replica Regions:** Replica regions are read-only copies of the data. You can perform read operations (queries and scans) on these replica regions, reducing read latency for users in those regions.

- **Conflict Resolution:** DynamoDB provides conflict resolution mechanisms to handle conflicts that may arise when updates occur simultaneously in different regions.

## 2. Creating a Global Table

To create a Global Table in DynamoDB, follow these steps:

1. Navigate to the DynamoDB console.
2. Select your table and click on the "Global Tables" tab.
3. Choose "Add region" to specify the replica regions.
4. Configure settings for each replica region, such as read capacity mode and encryption settings.
5. Click "Create Global Table."

Once created, DynamoDB handles data replication, ensuring that changes made in the primary region are propagated to replica regions with minimal replication lag.

### 3. Using Global Tables in Your Application

To use Global Tables in your application, follow these guidelines:

- For write operations, always direct them to the primary region. DynamoDB automatically replicates changes to replica regions.

- For read operations, you can choose to read from the primary region or a replica region. Reading from a nearby replica region can reduce read latency for users in that region.

- Be aware of conflict resolution strategies. DynamoDB offers "last writer wins" and "custom resolution" options to handle conflicts in multi-region writes.

### 4. Code Example

Here's an example of using the AWS SDK for Python (Boto3) to perform read operations on a Global Table:

```
import boto3
```

```
# Initialize DynamoDB client

dynamodb = boto3.client('dynamodb')

# Specify the Global Table name

table_name = 'MyGlobalTable'

# Choose a replica region endpoint

replica_region_endpoint = 'dynamodb.us-west-2.amazonaws.com'

# Perform a read operation in the replica region

response = dynamodb.get_item(

TableName=table_name,

Key={'PrimaryKey': {'S': 'example-key'}},

**{'RegionName': 'us-west-2', 'EndpointUrl': replica_region_endpoint}

)

# Process the response data

item = response.get('Item')

if item:

print("Item found:", item)

else:

print("Item not found.")
```

This code demonstrates how to read data from a replica region of a Global Table, which can help distribute read traffic and reduce latency for your global user base.

Global Tables in DynamoDB provide a robust solution for maintaining highly available and low-latency databases across multiple AWS regions, ensuring that your application can scale and perform reliably, even in the face of regional outages.

## Section 11.5: Using Time to Live (TTL) for Data Expiry

In this section, we will explore how to leverage Time to Live (TTL) functionality in Amazon DynamoDB to automatically expire and delete items from a table when they reach a specified expiration timestamp. This feature is particularly useful for managing data that has a limited lifespan, such as session data, temporary records, or cache entries.

### 1. Understanding TTL in DynamoDB

Time to Live (TTL) is a feature in DynamoDB that allows you to set a timestamp attribute for items in a table. When an item's TTL attribute expires (reaches the specified timestamp), DynamoDB automatically removes the item from the table. This eliminates the need for manual cleanup processes.

Key points about TTL in DynamoDB:

- **TTL Attribute:** To enable TTL for a table, you must define an attribute as the TTL attribute. This attribute should contain Unix timestamp values (in seconds) representing the expiration times.

- **Automatic Deletion:** DynamoDB periodically scans the table for expired items and removes them. This process is automatic and requires no manual intervention.

- **Soft Delete:** Items deleted by TTL are soft-deleted, which means they are removed from the table but still exist in backups and streams for a certain retention period.

## 2. Enabling TTL for a Table

To enable TTL for a DynamoDB table, follow these steps:

1. Open the DynamoDB console.
2. Select your table and click on the "Manage TTL" button.
3. Choose an attribute to use as the TTL attribute.
4. Specify the attribute's data type and confirm the retention policy (how long deleted items are kept).
5. Save the TTL configuration.

Once TTL is enabled, DynamoDB will take care of automatically expiring and deleting items that reach their specified expiration times.

## 3. Use Cases for TTL

TTL in DynamoDB can be beneficial for various use cases, including:

- **Session Management:** Automatically remove expired user sessions to free up resources.

- **Cache Invalidation:** Remove cached data after a certain period to ensure fresh data retrieval.

- **Temporary Data:** Delete temporary records or logs that are no longer needed.

- **Compliance Requirements:** Enforce data retention policies to meet compliance regulations.

## 4. Code Example

Here's an example of using the AWS SDK for Python (Boto3) to enable TTL for a DynamoDB table and insert items with TTL values:

```
import boto3

# Initialize DynamoDB client

dynamodb = boto3.client('dynamodb')

# Specify the table name

table_name = 'MyTTLTable'

# Enable TTL for the table

response = dynamodb.update_time_to_live(

TableName=table_name,

TimeToLiveSpecification={

'Enabled': True,

'AttributeName': 'ttl_timestamp' # Name of the TTL attribute

}

)
```

```
# Insert an item with a TTL value

response = dynamodb.put_item(

TableName=table_name,

Item={

'id': {'S': 'example-id'},

'data': {'S': 'example-data'},

'ttl_timestamp': {'N': '172800'} # TTL value for 2 days (in seconds)

}

)

print("TTL enabled and item inserted.")
```

This code demonstrates how to enable TTL for a table and insert an item with a TTL attribute. After 2 days, DynamoDB will automatically delete the item from the table.

Time to Live (TTL) functionality in DynamoDB simplifies the management of data expiration and deletion, allowing you to focus on building applications while ensuring that outdated data is automatically removed from your tables.

# Chapter 12: Troubleshooting and Maintenance

## Section 12.1: Identifying Common Issues in DynamoDB

In this section, we'll delve into the troubleshooting and maintenance aspects of Amazon DynamoDB. While DynamoDB is designed to be a highly available and managed service, it's essential to understand common issues and how to address them effectively.

### 1. Monitoring and Alarms

*Issue: Unusual High Throughput*

**Symptoms:** You observe a sudden spike in read or write throughput, leading to unexpected high costs.

**Possible Causes:**

- Increased application traffic.
- Misconfigured batch operations.

**Solution:**

- Monitor CloudWatch metrics for Read and Write Capacity Utilization.
- Set up CloudWatch Alarms to trigger when thresholds are exceeded.
- Investigate the root cause and optimize your application if necessary.

*Issue: Throttling Errors*

**Symptoms:** Applications start receiving ProvisionedThroughputExceededException errors.

**Possible Causes:**

- Exceeding provisioned capacity.
- Uneven workload distribution.

**Solution:**

- Use Auto Scaling to automatically adjust capacity.
- Monitor your application's access patterns and distribute traffic evenly across partitions.

## 2. Backup and Restore

*Issue: Data Loss*

**Symptoms:** Critical data is accidentally deleted or overwritten.

**Possible Causes:**

- Human error.
- Application bugs.

**Solution:**

- Regularly back up your DynamoDB tables using on-demand backups or continuous backups.

- Implement versioning or data retention policies in your application to mitigate data loss risks.

*Issue: Restore Failures*

**Symptoms:** Restore operations fail or take longer than expected.

**Possible Causes:**

- Lack of sufficient resources during the restore process.
- Issues with source backups.

**Solution:**

- Ensure there are enough write capacity units available.
- Validate the integrity of your backups and try the restore again.

## 3. Performance Optimization

*Issue: Slow Queries*

**Symptoms:** Query or scan operations take longer than acceptable response times.

**Possible Causes:**

- Inefficient data models.
- Unoptimized queries.

**Solution:**

- Review and optimize your data model.

- Use secondary indexes and projection expressions.
- Utilize query filters to reduce result sizes.

*Issue: High Latency*

**Symptoms:** High response times from DynamoDB.

**Possible Causes:**

- Network issues.
- Overloaded queries.

**Solution:**

- Monitor network performance and resolve any issues.
- Optimize your queries, and consider using DynamoDB Accelerator (DAX) for caching.

## 4. Logging and Monitoring

*Issue: Lack of Visibility*

**Symptoms:** Inadequate insight into system behavior.

**Possible Causes:**

- Insufficient logging and monitoring setup.

**Solution:**

- Implement detailed logging using CloudWatch Logs.

- Set up custom CloudWatch Alarms to monitor critical metrics.
- Use AWS X-Ray for tracing and diagnostics.

### 5. Conclusion

Effective troubleshooting and maintenance are crucial for ensuring the reliability and performance of your DynamoDB-based applications. Regularly monitor your tables, set up alarms, and be prepared to take action when issues arise. Additionally, having a well-defined backup and restore strategy can safeguard your data against unexpected events.

## Section 12.2: Effective Logging and Monitoring Strategies

In this section, we'll explore effective logging and monitoring strategies for Amazon DynamoDB. Robust logging and monitoring are essential for gaining insights into the health and performance of your DynamoDB applications. They help you identify issues, troubleshoot problems, and optimize your database usage.

### 1. CloudWatch Metrics

Amazon CloudWatch is a comprehensive monitoring service that provides valuable metrics for DynamoDB. By utilizing CloudWatch, you can gain visibility into various aspects of your DynamoDB tables, including:

- **Read and Write Capacity Utilization:** Monitor the consumption of your provisioned capacity to identify potential bottlenecks or over-provisioning.

- **Throttling Metrics:** Keep an eye on ThrottleRequests and ThrottleEvents to detect when your applications are being throttled due to exceeding provisioned capacity.

- **Errors and Latency:** Track error rates and latency metrics to identify performance issues and error-prone operations.

- **Consumed Read and Write Capacity:** Understand how much of your provisioned capacity is being consumed and whether it aligns with your application's requirements.

You can create CloudWatch Alarms based on these metrics to receive notifications when certain thresholds are breached, allowing you to take timely action.

## 2. CloudWatch Logs

CloudWatch Logs enables you to capture and store log data from your DynamoDB applications. You can set up logging at various levels, including:

- **Table-level Logging:** Enable logging for specific DynamoDB tables to capture data modifications and access patterns.

- **Application-level Logging:** Implement detailed logging within your application code to track specific actions, errors, and events.

By centralizing your logs in CloudWatch Logs, you can:

- **Perform Log Analysis:** Use CloudWatch Logs Insights to query and analyze log data to identify issues or trends.

- **Set Up Log Retention:** Configure log retention policies to manage your log data effectively.

## 3. AWS X-Ray Integration

AWS X-Ray is a distributed tracing service that can help you gain insights into the performance and behavior of your DynamoDB applications. By instrumenting your application code, you can trace requests as they traverse through different components, including DynamoDB.

Key benefits of using AWS X-Ray with DynamoDB include:

- **End-to-End Tracing:** Understand how requests flow through your application and identify bottlenecks.

- **Performance Analysis:** Analyze the time spent on individual DynamoDB operations to optimize queries.

- **Error Tracing:** Detect errors and exceptions in your DynamoDB interactions.

## 4. Custom Application Metrics

While CloudWatch provides a wealth of predefined metrics, you may need to track custom application-specific metrics. To achieve this, you can use the AWS SDKs and instrument your code to emit custom metrics.

For example, you can track:

- **Throughput:** Measure the number of read and write operations your application performs per second.

- **Query Performance:** Record query response times and track how they change over time.

- **Resource Utilization:** Monitor the memory, CPU, and network utilization of your application servers.

By collecting and visualizing these custom metrics, you can gain deeper insights into your DynamoDB application's performance.

## 5. Automation and Alerts

To effectively manage logging and monitoring, consider setting up automated processes and alerts:

- **Automated Log Retention:** Implement automated log retention policies to ensure you retain logs for the required duration without manual intervention.

- **Alerting:** Configure CloudWatch Alarms to notify your operations team or developers when specific thresholds are exceeded, such as high error rates or throttling events.

## 6. Conclusion

Implementing effective logging and monitoring strategies for your Amazon DynamoDB applications is crucial for maintaining their reliability, performance, and security. By leveraging CloudWatch, CloudWatch Logs, AWS X-Ray, custom application metrics, and automation, you can gain valuable insights, detect issues early, and take proactive measures to optimize your DynamoDB usage.

# Section 12.3: Performance Tuning and Bottleneck Analysis

In this section, we will delve into performance tuning and bottleneck analysis for Amazon DynamoDB. Achieving optimal performance is essential to ensure that your applications running on DynamoDB deliver a responsive and efficient user experience. We will explore strategies for identifying and addressing bottlenecks that may impact your DynamoDB workloads.

## 1. Identifying Performance Bottlenecks

Before you can optimize the performance of your DynamoDB application, it's crucial to identify bottlenecks. Common bottlenecks in DynamoDB workloads include:

- **Provisioned Throughput:** In provisioned capacity mode, if your tables are consistently consuming all of their provisioned capacity, you may experience throttling and performance degradation.

- **Hot Partitions:** DynamoDB partitions your data across multiple physical storage nodes. Hot partitions occur when a single partition receives a disproportionately high volume of requests, leading to uneven distribution and reduced performance.

- **Inefficient Queries:** Poorly designed queries that fetch large amounts of data or require extensive filtering can lead to high read or write costs and slow performance.

- **Large Items:** Storing excessively large items can impact read and write latencies, especially if these items frequently need to be accessed or modified.

## 2. Addressing Bottlenecks

Once you've identified bottlenecks, you can take specific actions to address them:

- **Provisioned Throughput Scaling:** If you encounter consistent throttling, consider adjusting your provisioned throughput settings. You can increase the provisioned capacity to handle higher traffic or use on-demand capacity mode for automatic scaling.

- **Partition Key Design:** Revisit your table's partition key design to distribute data evenly across partitions. Avoid using a partition key with high write or read traffic.

- **Query Optimization:** Analyze and optimize your queries to reduce the amount of data retrieved and processed. Use appropriate indexes to support efficient query patterns.

- **Item Size Reduction:** Minimize item size by removing unnecessary attributes or splitting large items into smaller ones. Smaller items generally lead to faster read and write operations.

## 3. Load Testing and Profiling

Load testing is a valuable technique for assessing your DynamoDB application's performance under various traffic scenarios. By simulating heavy workloads, you can identify how your application behaves under stress and whether bottlenecks emerge.

Profiling tools and techniques can help you pinpoint performance bottlenecks in your application code. You can use profilers to identify which parts of your code consume the most resources or exhibit suboptimal behavior.

## 4. Monitoring and Alerting

Continuously monitor your DynamoDB application's performance using CloudWatch metrics and alarms. Set up alarms for key metrics such as consumed read and write capacity, error rates, and latency. When an alarm triggers, it can notify your team, allowing for prompt investigation and action.

## 5. Testing Changes Safely

Before implementing changes to address bottlenecks, perform thorough testing in a staging or development environment. Changes can include modifying provisioned throughput settings, adjusting data models, or optimizing queries. Testing helps ensure that your optimizations have the desired effect without introducing regressions or new issues.

## 6. Conclusion

Performance tuning and bottleneck analysis are ongoing processes in Amazon DynamoDB application development. Regularly monitor your application, identify performance bottlenecks, and implement optimizations as needed to maintain the desired level of performance and responsiveness for your users. By proactively addressing bottlenecks, you can ensure that your DynamoDB workloads deliver a reliable and efficient experience.

## Section 12.4: Regular Maintenance and Health Checks

In this section, we'll explore the importance of regular maintenance and health checks for your Amazon DynamoDB tables and applications. Maintenance activities help ensure the long-term reliability and performance of your DynamoDB workloads.

### 1. Table and Index Optimization

One of the key aspects of regular maintenance is optimizing your DynamoDB tables and indexes. You should periodically review your data models, indexes, and access patterns to make necessary adjustments. Here are some maintenance tasks to consider:

- **Index Maintenance:** Review the usage of Local Secondary Indexes (LSIs) and Global Secondary Indexes (GSIs). Remove unused indexes to reduce write costs and storage.

- **Data Cleanup:** Identify and remove obsolete or unused data to keep your table size manageable. DynamoDB's Time to Live (TTL) feature can help automate data expiration.

- **Item Size Analysis:** Keep an eye on the size of your items. If you notice items growing significantly over time, consider strategies to reduce item size.

- **Query Optimization:** Periodically analyze your query patterns and optimize them for efficiency. Ensure that you're using the right indexes and query patterns.

## 2. Backups and Restore Testing

Regularly back up your DynamoDB tables to protect against data loss. Use on-demand backups or enable continuous backups for point-in-time recovery. Additionally, perform periodic restore testing to ensure that you can recover data when needed.

## 3. Monitoring and Alerts

Continuous monitoring is crucial for identifying issues early. Set up CloudWatch alarms to track metrics such as consumed capacity, latency, and error rates. When an alarm triggers, investigate the root cause and take corrective action promptly.

## 4. Performance Testing

Periodically conduct performance testing to assess the behavior of your DynamoDB workloads under different conditions. This testing helps you understand how your application performs as it scales and whether any bottlenecks emerge.

## 5. Security Audits

Perform security audits to ensure that your DynamoDB tables are protected against unauthorized access. Review and update IAM policies, fine-tune permissions, and conduct access reviews to maintain a secure environment.

## 6. Cost Optimization

Regularly analyze your DynamoDB costs and look for opportunities to optimize expenses. Consider using the AWS Cost Explorer to gain insights into your spending patterns and identify areas for cost reduction.

### 7. Patch Management

If you're using DynamoDB with other AWS services or libraries, stay up-to-date with software updates and patches. Keeping your dependencies current helps mitigate security vulnerabilities and ensures compatibility with the latest features and improvements.

### 8. Documentation and Knowledge Sharing

Maintain up-to-date documentation that describes your DynamoDB tables, data models, access patterns, and operational procedures. Share this knowledge with your team to ensure consistent best practices and troubleshooting procedures.

### 9. Disaster Recovery Testing

Periodically test your disaster recovery procedures to ensure that you can recover from catastrophic events. This testing includes scenarios like table restoration, data replication, and application failover.

### 10. Conclusion

Regular maintenance and health checks are essential to the long-term success of your Amazon DynamoDB deployments. By investing time and effort into these activities, you can ensure that your DynamoDB tables and applications remain reliable, secure, and cost-effective. Regular maintenance not only prevents issues but also prepares you to respond effectively when unexpected challenges arise.

---

## Section 12.5: Upgrading and Migrating Data

As technology evolves, it's essential to keep your Amazon DynamoDB environment up to date with the latest features and improvements. In this section, we'll discuss the importance of upgrading and migrating data in DynamoDB and provide guidelines for a smooth transition.

## 1. Why Upgrade?

Upgrading your DynamoDB resources can offer several benefits, including enhanced performance, new features, bug fixes, and security patches. AWS regularly releases updates to DynamoDB to improve its capabilities and address potential vulnerabilities.

## 2. Types of Upgrades

There are two primary types of upgrades in DynamoDB:

- **Software Upgrades:** These upgrades involve updating the DynamoDB software to the latest version. AWS handles the maintenance of the software, ensuring that you receive the latest bug fixes and features automatically.

- **Capacity Upgrades:** When your workload demands change, you might need to upgrade your provisioned capacity settings. This could involve increasing read and write capacity units to handle higher traffic or scaling down to save costs during low-traffic periods.

## 3. Planning the Upgrade

Before initiating an upgrade, it's crucial to plan carefully:

- **Review Release Notes:** Check AWS release notes to understand what changes and improvements each update brings. This helps you determine if the upgrade aligns with your requirements.

- **Test in Staging:** Whenever possible, test the upgrade in a staging environment that mirrors your production environment. This allows you to identify and resolve any issues before applying the upgrade to your production resources.

- **Backup Data:** Take backups of your DynamoDB tables before performing any major upgrade or migration. This ensures that you can recover your data if anything goes wrong during the process.

- **Check Compatibility:** Verify that any third-party libraries, SDKs, or applications interacting with DynamoDB are compatible with the upgraded version.

## 4. Performing the Upgrade

The steps to perform an upgrade will vary depending on the type of upgrade you're undertaking:

- **Software Upgrade:** AWS typically manages software upgrades automatically. You can opt for automated or manual control based on your preference. For manual control, you can schedule the upgrade during a maintenance window to minimize disruption.

- **Capacity Upgrade:** If you need to adjust provisioned capacity settings, you can do so using the AWS Management Console, AWS CLI, or SDKs. Be cautious when scaling down, as it may lead to insufficient capacity during traffic spikes.

## 5. Monitoring and Validation

After an upgrade, closely monitor your DynamoDB resources for any unexpected behavior. Use CloudWatch alarms to set up automated notifications for specific metrics, such as error rates or latency.

Perform thorough testing to validate that your applications and workloads continue to function correctly with the upgraded DynamoDB environment.

## 6. Rollback Plan

Always have a rollback plan in case the upgrade encounters unforeseen issues. This plan should include steps to revert to the previous configuration, restore data, and address any impact on your application's functionality.

## 7. Conclusion

Upgrading and migrating data in Amazon DynamoDB is a routine part of maintaining a healthy and efficient database environment. By planning upgrades carefully, testing in controlled environments, and having contingency plans, you can ensure a smooth transition to new DynamoDB versions and configurations while minimizing the risk of disruptions to your applications. Regular upgrades help you take full advantage of DynamoDB's capabilities and security enhancements.

# Chapter 13: Best Practices in DynamoDB Usage

## Section 13.1: Design Patterns for DynamoDB

Amazon DynamoDB offers a wide range of design patterns and strategies to optimize your database for various use cases. In this section, we'll explore some best practices and design patterns for DynamoDB that can help you make the most of this NoSQL database service.

### 1. Single Table Design

One of the fundamental design patterns in DynamoDB is the Single Table Design. Instead of using multiple tables for different entities, you can often store all your data in a single table. This pattern is highly efficient and helps you avoid complex JOIN operations, making queries faster and more cost-effective.

### 2. Use of Composite Keys

Composite keys, which consist of a partition key and a sort key, allow you to create hierarchical data structures within a single table. This is useful for scenarios where you need to represent relationships between items. For example, in an e-commerce application, you can use a composite key to organize orders and items within those orders efficiently.

### 3. Secondary Indexes

Leverage secondary indexes (Local Secondary Indexes and Global Secondary Indexes) to enable flexible querying of your data. These indexes can help you retrieve data based on attributes other than the primary key. When designing your schema, carefully consider which attributes should be part of secondary indexes to support your query patterns.

## 4. Using Sparse Indexes

Sparse indexes are secondary indexes that are created conditionally. They only include items that meet specific criteria. This pattern can be handy when you want to optimize query performance for a subset of your data without incurring additional storage costs for non-relevant items.

## 5. Time-To-Live (TTL) for Data Expiry

DynamoDB offers TTL to automatically remove expired data from your table. This is beneficial for scenarios like caching or managing temporary data. By setting a TTL attribute for items, you can ensure that DynamoDB automatically deletes them when they are no longer needed, reducing storage costs.

## 6. Use of DynamoDB Streams

DynamoDB Streams capture changes to your table's data. You can use these streams to build real-time applications, trigger Lambda functions, and maintain an audit trail of changes. Design your applications to take advantage of DynamoDB Streams for various use cases, such as data synchronization, notifications, or analytics.

## 7. Data Consistency Models

Understand the data consistency models provided by DynamoDB, namely, eventually consistent reads and strongly consistent reads. Choose the appropriate consistency level for your application's requirements. Strongly consistent reads ensure the latest data, while eventually consistent reads are faster and offer cost savings.

## 8. Using DynamoDB Accelerator (DAX)

DynamoDB Accelerator (DAX) is an in-memory cache that can significantly improve read performance. Consider using DAX for read-heavy workloads to reduce the load on your DynamoDB tables and decrease read latency.

## 9. Best Practices for Batch Operations

When performing batch operations like BatchWriteItem or BatchGetItem, follow best practices to optimize throughput and minimize API call costs. Ensure your requests and responses are within DynamoDB's limits and leverage parallelism for improved performance.

## 10. Monitoring and Optimization

Regularly monitor your DynamoDB tables using Amazon CloudWatch metrics. Identify performance bottlenecks, adjust provisioned capacity as needed, and fine-tune your queries and indexing strategies. Optimization is an ongoing process to ensure efficient database operations.

By understanding and applying these design patterns and best practices, you can build highly efficient and cost-effective applications on Amazon DynamoDB, tailored to your specific use cases and workloads. DynamoDB's flexibility and scalability, combined with these patterns, enable you to achieve optimal performance and reliability in your NoSQL database deployments.

# Section 13.2: Data Consistency and

# Concurrency Control

When working with Amazon DynamoDB, it's crucial to understand data consistency and how to handle concurrency control to ensure the integrity of your data. In this section, we'll explore the concepts of data consistency and concurrency control in DynamoDB.

## 1. Eventual Consistency vs. Strong Consistency

DynamoDB offers two consistency models for read operations: eventual consistency and strong consistency. Eventual consistency ensures that, after a write, all subsequent read requests will eventually return the latest version of the data. This consistency model is suitable for applications where slight delays in seeing the most up-to-date data are acceptable.

On the other hand, strong consistency guarantees that every read request will return the most recent write. However, strong consistency may have a performance impact, especially during periods of high write activity.

To achieve strong consistency in DynamoDB, you can use the ConsistentRead parameter when making read requests. For example, when using the AWS SDK for DynamoDB in Python:

```
import boto3

# Initialize DynamoDB client

dynamodb = boto3.client('dynamodb')

# Perform a strongly consistent read

response = dynamodb.get_item(

TableName='YourTableName',
```

```
Key={
'PrimaryKey': {'N': '12345'}
},
ConsistentRead=True
)
```

## 2. Optimistic Concurrency Control

Optimistic concurrency control is a technique used to prevent conflicts when multiple clients attempt to update the same item simultaneously. DynamoDB supports optimistic concurrency control by providing a version number attribute called the "Version Number" or "Versioning."

Here's a simplified example in Python:

```python
import boto3
# Initialize DynamoDB client
dynamodb = boto3.client('dynamodb')
# Define the key of the item to be updated
key = {'PrimaryKey': {'N': '12345'}}
# Get the current item
response = dynamodb.get_item(
TableName='YourTableName',
Key=key
)
```

```
# Extract the current version number
current_version = response['Item']['Version']['N']
# Prepare the updated item with the incremented version
updated_item = {
'PrimaryKey': {'N': '12345'},
'Version': {'N': str(int(current_version) + 1)},
# Other attributes to update
}
# Use a conditional update to ensure version consistency
dynamodb.update_item(
TableName='YourTableName',
Key=key,
UpdateExpression='SET #version = :new_version',
ExpressionAttributeNames={'#version': 'Version'},
ExpressionAttributeValues={':new_version': {'N': updated_item['Version']['N']}},
ConditionExpression='#version = :current_version',
ReturnValues='ALL_NEW'
)
```

In this example, we first retrieve the current version of the item, increment it, and then use a conditional update to ensure that the item is only updated if the version number hasn't changed since we retrieved it. If another client has already updated the item, the conditional expression will fail, preventing conflicts.

### 3. Pessimistic Concurrency Control

Pessimistic concurrency control is another approach where locks are used to prevent multiple clients from modifying the same data simultaneously. DynamoDB does not provide built-in support for pessimistic concurrency control, so you would need to implement it yourself using other AWS services or external mechanisms if your application requires it.

### 4. Handling Conflicts

When conflicts occur due to concurrent updates, it's essential to have a conflict resolution strategy in place. This strategy could involve automatically retrying the update, notifying the user, or merging conflicting changes based on your application's requirements.

By understanding and implementing appropriate data consistency and concurrency control mechanisms, you can ensure the reliability and correctness of your DynamoDB applications, even in scenarios with high concurrent access and frequent updates.

---

## Section 13.3: Cost-Effective Strategies for DynamoDB

Managing costs effectively is a crucial aspect of using Amazon DynamoDB. While DynamoDB offers excellent performance and scalability, it's essential to optimize your usage to ensure cost efficiency. In this section, we'll explore several strategies and best practices for cost-effective DynamoDB usage.

## 1. Use On-Demand Capacity Mode Wisely

DynamoDB provides two capacity modes: On-Demand and Provisioned. The On-Demand capacity mode charges you for the actual read and write requests you make, making it suitable for applications with varying workloads. However, for predictable workloads or high-throughput scenarios, Provisioned capacity can be more cost-effective.

When choosing between On-Demand and Provisioned capacity, analyze your application's usage patterns and predictability. You can switch between these capacity modes as your requirements change, providing flexibility and cost optimization.

## 2. Implement Data Retention Policies

To control costs, implement data retention policies that define how long you keep data in DynamoDB. Use the Time to Live (TTL) feature to automatically delete items that are no longer needed after a specified period. This prevents unnecessary storage costs for outdated data.

Here's how you can enable TTL for a table:

```
import boto3

# Initialize DynamoDB client

dynamodb = boto3.client('dynamodb')

# Enable TTL for a table (replace 'YourTableName' with your table name)

dynamodb.update_time_to_live(

TableName='YourTableName',
```

```
TimeToLiveSpecification={
'Enabled': True,
'AttributeName': 'ttl_attribute_name'
}
)
```

## 3. Use Sparse Indexes

Sparse indexes are secondary indexes that only include items where the index key exists. By using sparse indexes, you can reduce the number of read and write capacity units required for your secondary index, resulting in cost savings.

Ensure that you create indexes only for attributes that are frequently used for querying to avoid unnecessary costs associated with maintaining additional indexes.

## 4. Monitor and Adjust Provisioned Throughput

If you are using Provisioned capacity mode, regularly monitor your table's performance and adjust provisioned throughput based on actual usage. DynamoDB provides auto-scaling options that can automatically adjust capacity to match your workload, reducing costs during periods of low activity.

## 5. Optimize Query and Scan Operations

Efficiently design your queries to minimize the amount of data you retrieve. Use projection expressions to limit the attributes returned in query results, reducing read costs. Avoid using Scan operations unless necessary, as they can consume a large number of read capacity units.

### 6. Leverage Reserved Capacity

If your application has predictable and consistent traffic patterns, consider purchasing reserved capacity for DynamoDB. This option can significantly reduce your long-term costs by offering substantial discounts in exchange for a commitment to a specific level of provisioned capacity.

### 7. Clean Up Unused Resources

Regularly review and clean up unused tables, indexes, and other resources. Unused resources can accumulate costs over time, so ensure that you have a process in place to identify and decommission them.

### 8. Cost Allocation and Monitoring

Leverage AWS Cost Explorer and AWS Cost and Usage Reports to monitor and analyze your DynamoDB costs. Implement cost allocation tags to attribute costs to specific resources or teams within your organization.

By implementing these cost-effective strategies and regularly reviewing your DynamoDB usage, you can optimize your costs while still benefiting from the power and scalability that DynamoDB offers for your applications.

---

## Section 13.4: Planning for Scalability and Growth

Scalability is a fundamental aspect of Amazon DynamoDB, ensuring that your database can handle increasing workloads and data volumes. In this section, we will explore best practices for planning and preparing your DynamoDB setup to accommodate growth.

## 1. Choose the Right Partition Key

One of the key decisions when designing your DynamoDB tables is selecting an appropriate partition key. The partition key determines how data is distributed across multiple storage nodes, impacting the database's scalability. A poorly chosen partition key can lead to "hot" partitions with excessive read/write activity, causing throttling and performance issues.

To choose an effective partition key:

- Select a high-cardinality attribute (one with many distinct values) to evenly distribute data.
- Avoid using attributes with a limited set of values, as this can lead to uneven data distribution.
- Consider using composite keys (partition key and sort key) to distribute data more evenly and support various query patterns.

## 2. Monitor and Auto-Scaling

DynamoDB provides auto-scaling options for provisioned capacity mode, allowing your tables to automatically adjust their capacity to match the workload. Regularly monitor your table's performance metrics, such as consumed read and write capacity units, and enable auto-scaling to ensure your database can handle increased traffic without manual intervention.

## 3. Use On-Demand Capacity Mode

If your workload is unpredictable or experiences significant fluctuations, consider using DynamoDB's On-Demand capacity mode. It eliminates the need to provision read and write capacity in advance, automatically scaling to accommodate your application's needs. While this mode can be more cost-effective for sporadic workloads, it may not be suitable for highly predictable workloads.

## 4. Implement Caching

Integrate caching mechanisms like Amazon DynamoDB Accelerator (DAX) or in-memory caches to reduce the load on your DynamoDB tables. Caching can help serve frequently accessed data quickly and reduce the number of requests reaching your database, leading to lower read and write costs.

## 5. Data Archiving and Cleanup

Implement data archiving and cleanup strategies to manage older or less frequently accessed data. Use Time to Live (TTL) to automatically delete expired items and periodically archive or migrate data to lower-cost storage solutions like Amazon S3.

## 6. Leverage Global Tables

If your application requires high availability across multiple geographic regions, consider using DynamoDB Global Tables. This feature replicates your data across multiple AWS regions, allowing you to provide low-latency access to users worldwide while ensuring data durability. This is especially useful for applications with global user bases and high scalability requirements.

## 7. Disaster Recovery Planning

Plan for disaster recovery by regularly creating backups of your DynamoDB tables and storing them in a secure location. Familiarize yourself with AWS's disaster recovery services like AWS Backup and practice restoring data from backups to ensure you can recover quickly in case of data loss or system failures.

### 8. Capacity Planning

Regularly review and adjust your provisioned capacity to align with your application's growth. Amazon CloudWatch can help you analyze historical data and make informed decisions about capacity provisioning. Remember that over-provisioning can lead to unnecessary costs, while under-provisioning can result in poor performance.

By carefully planning for scalability and growth and implementing these best practices, you can ensure that your DynamoDB-powered applications can handle increased workloads and data volumes while maintaining performance and cost efficiency.

---

## Section 13.5: Tips for Efficient Data Retrieval

Efficient data retrieval is crucial for maintaining the performance of your Amazon DynamoDB applications. In this section, we'll explore some tips and best practices to optimize the retrieval of data from DynamoDB tables.

### 1. Use Query Instead of Scan

When retrieving data from DynamoDB, prefer using the Query operation over Scan whenever possible. Query is designed for retrieving specific items based on their primary key attributes, making it more efficient and predictable. In contrast, Scan scans the entire table, which can be slow and costly for large datasets.

```
# Example Query operation in Python using Boto3
```

```
response = table.query(
KeyConditionExpression=Key('partition_key').eq('value')
)
```

## 2. Utilize Indexes

DynamoDB allows you to create secondary indexes (Local Secondary Indexes or Global Secondary Indexes) to improve query performance. Use indexes for common query patterns that involve non-key attributes. Indexes enable efficient filtering and sorting of data.

```
# Example of querying using a Global Secondary Index (GSI)
response = table.query(
IndexName='your_index_name',
KeyConditionExpression=Key('indexed_attribute').eq('value')
)
```

## 3. Select Only Necessary Attributes

When querying or scanning, use the ProjectionExpression parameter to specify which attributes you need in the result. Retrieving only the required attributes can reduce the amount of data transferred and improve query performance.

```
# Example of selecting specific attributes in a query
response = table.query(
KeyConditionExpression=Key('partition_key').eq('value'),
ProjectionExpression='attribute1, attribute2'
```

```
)
```

## 4. Use BatchGetItem for Multiple Items

If you need to retrieve multiple items by their primary keys, use the BatchGetItem operation. This allows you to fetch up to 100 items in a single request, reducing the number of round-trip calls to DynamoDB.

```
# Example BatchGetItem operation in Python using Boto3
response = client.batch_get_item(
RequestItems={
'TableName': {
'Keys': [
{'partition_key': 'key1'},
{'partition_key': 'key2'},
# Add more keys as needed
]
}
}
)
```

## 5. Avoid Large Query Result Sets

Be cautious when querying or scanning for a large number of items, as it can impact performance and consume a significant amount of provisioned capacity. Consider paginating results and using filters to narrow down the dataset.

### 6. Monitor and Optimize Queries

Regularly monitor your application's query performance using Amazon CloudWatch or DynamoDB's built-in metrics. Identify slow or resource-intensive queries and optimize them by adjusting your data model or index strategies.

### 7. Use Query Filters Sparingly

While DynamoDB supports filtering results using the FilterExpression parameter, it's essential to use filters sparingly. Filtering is applied after the initial data retrieval, potentially leading to higher read costs and slower query performance. Whenever possible, design your data model and queries to avoid the need for post-query filtering.

By following these tips for efficient data retrieval in Amazon DynamoDB, you can ensure that your applications deliver fast and cost-effective access to your data, even as your dataset grows.

---

# Chapter 14: Case Studies and Real-World Applications

In this chapter, we will delve into various case studies and real-world applications that showcase the versatility and effectiveness of Amazon DynamoDB in solving real-world challenges. DynamoDB has been adopted by organizations across different industries to power mission-critical systems, and these case studies provide insights into how it is used to address specific use cases and achieve scalable and reliable solutions.

## Section 14.1: E-commerce Platforms and DynamoDB

E-commerce platforms are known for their dynamic and high-traffic nature, making them an ideal use case for Amazon DynamoDB. Let's explore how DynamoDB is employed in the e-commerce industry to support features like product catalog management, user profiles, real-time inventory tracking, and order processing.

### *1. Product Catalog Management*

In e-commerce, managing a vast catalog of products with varying attributes can be challenging. DynamoDB's flexible schema allows e-commerce platforms to efficiently store and query product data. Each product can be represented as an item in the table, and attributes like product name, description, price, and availability can be stored as attributes.

```
{
"product_id": "12345",
"name": "Smartphone",
"description": "High-end smartphone with advanced features",
"price": 599.99,
"available_quantity": 100
}
```

*2. User Profiles and Personalization*

E-commerce platforms use DynamoDB to manage user profiles and preferences. User data, such as purchase history, favorite products, and browsing behavior, can be stored in DynamoDB. This information is used to provide personalized recommendations, improving the user experience and increasing conversion rates.

```
{
"user_id": "user123",
"name": "John Doe",
"email": "john@example.com",
"favorites": ["12345", "67890"],
"purchase_history": ["order1", "order2"]
}
```

*3. Real-time Inventory Tracking*

Maintaining accurate inventory levels is critical for e-commerce. DynamoDB allows platforms to track inventory in real-time, ensuring that products are available when customers want to purchase them. Developers can use conditional updates to atomically adjust inventory levels during order processing.

```
# Python code for updating inventory in DynamoDB
response = table.update_item(
Key={'product_id': '12345'},
```

```
UpdateExpression='SET available_quantity = available_quantity - :qty',

ExpressionAttributeValues={':qty': 1},

ConditionExpression='available_quantity >= :qty'

)
```

### *4. Order Processing and Transaction Support*

E-commerce platforms handle a large number of orders daily. DynamoDB's support for transactions ensures that order processing is reliable and maintains data consistency. In case of failures, transactions can be rolled back to prevent incomplete orders.

```
# Python code for processing an order with DynamoDB transaction

with table.batch_writer() as batch:

batch.put_item(Item={'order_id': 'order123', 'status': 'processing'})

batch.put_item(Item={'order_id': 'order123', 'status': 'shipped'})
```

### *5. Scalability for Flash Sales and Seasonal Peaks*

E-commerce platforms often experience traffic spikes during flash sales and holiday seasons. DynamoDB's auto-scaling feature enables platforms to handle increased demand automatically without manual intervention, ensuring a seamless shopping experience for customers.

These case studies highlight how Amazon DynamoDB plays a pivotal role in ensuring the performance, scalability, and reliability of e-commerce platforms. Its ability to handle large volumes of data and deliver low-latency responses makes it a preferred choice for businesses operating in the highly competitive e-commerce landscape. In the next sections, we will explore more real-world applications and case studies across various domains.

## Section 14.2: Implementing IoT Solutions

The Internet of Things (IoT) has gained immense popularity, with a wide range of devices and sensors generating data that needs to be collected, processed, and analyzed in real-time. Amazon DynamoDB serves as a robust and scalable backend for IoT applications, allowing businesses to ingest, store, and query vast amounts of IoT data efficiently.

### IoT Data Ingestion

One of the fundamental aspects of IoT solutions is data ingestion from devices. These devices, such as sensors, wearables, and smart appliances, continuously send data to the cloud for processing. DynamoDB's high write throughput and low-latency capabilities make it an excellent choice for handling real-time data streams.

#### *Storing Sensor Data*

Consider a scenario where temperature and humidity sensors in a smart greenhouse send data to DynamoDB. Each sensor reading can be stored as an item in a DynamoDB table, with attributes representing timestamp, sensor ID, temperature, and humidity values.

```
{
"timestamp": "2024-02-10T14:30:00Z",
```

"sensor_id": "sensor123",

"temperature": 25.5,

"humidity": 60.2

}

## Real-time Analytics

IoT solutions often require real-time analytics to derive insights from incoming data. DynamoDB integrates seamlessly with AWS services like AWS Lambda and Amazon Kinesis for real-time data processing.

### *Lambda Triggers*

AWS Lambda can be configured to trigger functions whenever new data arrives in a DynamoDB table. This serverless architecture allows you to perform real-time analysis, notifications, or data transformations as data is ingested.

```
# Python code for a Lambda function triggered by DynamoDB
def lambda_handler(event, context):
for record in event['Records']:
# Perform real-time analysis or actions based on the record
```

## Scalability for IoT Growth

IoT solutions often experience rapid growth in the number of devices and data volume. DynamoDB's auto-scaling feature ensures that your database can handle increased data ingestion without manual intervention.

### Time-Series Data and Retention Policies

In IoT, time-series data is prevalent, and managing data retention policies is crucial. DynamoDB's Time to Live (TTL) feature enables automatic removal of outdated data, reducing storage costs.

### Device Management

DynamoDB can be used for device management, storing metadata, and configurations for IoT devices. Each device can have its own item in the table, making it easy to update settings and monitor device health.

### Security and Access Control

IoT data often contains sensitive information. DynamoDB provides robust security features, including AWS Identity and Access Management (IAM) roles and fine-grained access control, to ensure data confidentiality and integrity.

Implementing IoT solutions with Amazon DynamoDB allows businesses to harness the power of real-time data analytics, scalability, and data retention management. Whether it's monitoring environmental conditions in smart agriculture or tracking equipment in industrial settings, DynamoDB provides a reliable foundation for IoT applications.

## Section 14.3: Building Scalable Mobile Backends

Mobile applications have become an integral part of our daily lives, and building scalable and reliable backends is crucial for providing a seamless user experience. Amazon DynamoDB offers a powerful solution for building mobile backends that can handle high traffic, deliver low-latency responses, and ensure data durability.

## Mobile Backend Architecture

When designing a mobile backend, it's essential to consider factors like user authentication, data storage, and real-time data synchronization. DynamoDB can serve as the backbone of your mobile backend, supporting various features:

### *User Authentication*

Amazon Cognito, an AWS service, provides robust user authentication and identity management. You can integrate Amazon Cognito with DynamoDB to securely store user profiles and credentials. DynamoDB's fine-grained access control allows you to define who can access which data.

### *Data Storage*

DynamoDB tables can store user-generated content, app settings, and other data. It excels at handling structured and semi-structured data, making it suitable for a wide range of mobile applications.

### *Real-Time Data Synchronization*

For real-time data synchronization across devices, DynamoDB Streams can be leveraged. Whenever data in a DynamoDB table changes, the corresponding DynamoDB Stream can trigger AWS Lambda functions to propagate updates to connected mobile clients through WebSockets or other communication protocols.

## Offline Support

Mobile applications often need to work offline or in unreliable network conditions. DynamoDB provides offline support through AWS Mobile SDKs. With this feature, users can interact with the app even when they have no network connectivity. When the network is restored, changes made offline can be synchronized with the server.

## Push Notifications

Engaging users through push notifications is a common mobile app feature. AWS Simple Notification Service (SNS) can be used to send push notifications to mobile devices based on events in your DynamoDB tables. For example, you can notify users of new messages, updates, or other relevant information.

## Scalability and Auto-Scaling

As mobile apps grow in popularity, the backend infrastructure must scale to meet increasing demand. DynamoDB's auto-scaling feature ensures that your database can handle the growing number of users and data without manual intervention.

## Performance Monitoring

To ensure optimal performance of your mobile backend, you can use Amazon CloudWatch to monitor DynamoDB's metrics, such as request latency, consumed capacity, and error rates. This monitoring helps you identify bottlenecks and optimize your application's performance.

### Security

Security is paramount in mobile app development. DynamoDB integrates seamlessly with AWS Identity and Access Management (IAM) for access control. You can enforce data privacy and security by defining fine-grained access policies.

In summary, Amazon DynamoDB serves as a robust and scalable backend for mobile applications. It provides the necessary components for user authentication, data storage, real-time synchronization, offline support, push notifications, scalability, performance monitoring, and security. By leveraging DynamoDB's capabilities, you can focus on delivering a feature-rich and responsive mobile app while AWS manages the backend infrastructure.

## Section 14.4: Data Analytics and Reporting

Data analytics and reporting are essential components of modern businesses and applications. They help organizations make data-driven decisions, gain insights into user behavior, and track key performance indicators. Amazon DynamoDB, with its flexibility and scalability, can be a valuable data source for building analytics and reporting solutions.

### Design Considerations

When using DynamoDB for data analytics and reporting, consider the following design principles:

#### *1. Data Aggregation*

Aggregate data in DynamoDB to reduce the volume of data transferred and processed by your analytics system. You can use AWS

Lambda functions or other serverless services to perform real-time aggregation and store summarized data in a separate table.

*2. Indexes*

Leverage DynamoDB's Local Secondary Indexes (LSIs) and Global Secondary Indexes (GSIs) to optimize queries for reporting purposes. Create indexes on attributes commonly used in analytics queries to speed up data retrieval.

*3. Time-Based Data*

If your reporting involves time-based data, consider using time-based partitioning. Partition your data by date or time range to facilitate efficient querying for historical data. DynamoDB's Time to Live (TTL) feature can help automatically expire old data.

*4. Materialized Views*

Create materialized views of your data by precomputing aggregations or transformations and storing them in separate tables. This approach accelerates query performance for specific reporting requirements.

*5. Data Export*

To integrate DynamoDB data with popular analytics and reporting tools like Amazon QuickSight, Amazon Redshift, or third-party solutions, use data export features like DynamoDB Streams or AWS Data Pipeline. Exported data can be transformed and analyzed in these tools.

## Building Analytics with AWS Services

Amazon Web Services (AWS) provides various services that complement DynamoDB for building analytics and reporting solutions:

*1. Amazon Athena*

Amazon Athena is an interactive query service that allows you to analyze data stored in Amazon S3 using standard SQL queries. You can use Athena to query data exported from DynamoDB into S3.

*2. Amazon QuickSight*

Amazon QuickSight is a fully managed business intelligence service that enables you to create and publish interactive dashboards and reports. You can connect QuickSight to DynamoDB and build visualizations based on your data.

*3. AWS Glue*

AWS Glue is a managed extract, transform, and load (ETL) service that can automatically discover, catalog, and transform data from various sources, including DynamoDB. It can prepare data for analytics and reporting.

*4. Amazon Redshift*

Amazon Redshift is a fully managed data warehouse service that can be used to analyze large volumes of data efficiently. You can export data from DynamoDB to Redshift for more complex analytics.

## Sample Code

Here's an example of how you can use the AWS SDK for Python (Boto3) to export data from DynamoDB to Amazon S3 for further analysis with Amazon Athena:

```
import boto3

# Initialize DynamoDB and S3 clients

dynamodb = boto3.client('dynamodb')

s3 = boto3.client('s3')

# Specify DynamoDB table and S3 bucket

table_name = 'YourDynamoDBTable'

bucket_name = 'YourS3Bucket'

export_prefix = 'dynamodb-export/'

# Export data to S3

response = dynamodb.create_backup(

TableName=table_name,

BackupName='DynamoDBExport',

S3BucketName=bucket_name,

S3Prefix=export_prefix

)

# Wait for the export to complete

backup_arn = response['BackupDetails']['BackupArn']
```

```
dynamodb.get_waiter('backup_exists').wait(
BackupArn=backup_arn,
WaiterConfig={'Delay': 30, 'MaxAttempts': 60}
)
print('Data export completed.')
```

This code initiates a backup of your DynamoDB table and exports it to an S3 bucket, making it available for analysis using Athena or other analytics tools.

In conclusion, Amazon DynamoDB can be an excellent data source for building analytics and reporting solutions when coupled with AWS services like Athena, QuickSight, Glue, and Redshift. By following design best practices and leveraging AWS services, you can unlock valuable insights from your DynamoDB data.

---

## Section 14.5: Lessons from Large-Scale Deployments

Learning from large-scale deployments of Amazon DynamoDB can provide valuable insights and best practices for effectively managing and scaling NoSQL databases in production environments. In this section, we'll explore some of the key lessons and recommendations drawn from real-world scenarios.

### 1. Capacity Planning

One of the most critical aspects of DynamoDB deployment is capacity planning. It's essential to carefully estimate your read and write requirements and provision the appropriate capacity to handle your workload. Large-scale deployments often involve the use of on-demand capacity mode or auto-scaling to adapt to changing traffic patterns.

## 2. Data Modeling and Partitioning

Effective data modeling and partitioning are fundamental to DynamoDB's performance. Large-scale deployments benefit from well-designed partition keys that distribute data evenly across partitions. Using composite keys and secondary indexes strategically can optimize query performance.

## 3. Global Tables for Multi-Region Deployments

For high availability and disaster recovery, large-scale applications often use DynamoDB Global Tables to replicate data across multiple AWS regions. This ensures data availability even in the event of regional outages and minimizes latency for global users.

## 4. Time to Live (TTL) for Data Management

Using DynamoDB's Time to Live (TTL) feature is essential for managing data lifecycle and reducing storage costs. It automatically deletes expired items, making it an effective way to handle data retention policies.

## 5. Monitoring and Alarms

Implement robust monitoring and alerting mechanisms using Amazon CloudWatch. Set up alarms for key performance metrics, such as consumed read and write capacity units, to detect and respond to issues promptly.

### 6. Backup and Restore Strategies

Regularly backup your DynamoDB tables to protect against data loss and accidental deletions. Implement automated backup and restore strategies, and test them to ensure data recoverability.

### 7. Performance Optimization

Continuously monitor and optimize your DynamoDB tables for performance. Use tools like AWS Trusted Advisor and AWS Well-Architected to identify performance bottlenecks and inefficiencies.

### 8. Cost Optimization

Leverage DynamoDB's flexible pricing options, such as on-demand capacity mode and reserved capacity, to optimize costs. Implement cost allocation tags to track expenses effectively.

### 9. Security and Access Control

Implement strong security measures, including IAM roles and policies, to control access to your DynamoDB resources. Regularly review and update permissions to follow the principle of least privilege.

### 10. Disaster Recovery Planning

Develop comprehensive disaster recovery plans and perform regular drills to ensure your application can recover from various failure scenarios. Consider using AWS Backup for automated data protection.

## 11. Load Testing and Performance Tuning

Conduct load testing to simulate real-world traffic conditions and identify performance bottlenecks. Performance tuning may involve adjusting provisioned capacity, optimizing queries, and fine-tuning table designs.

## 12. Compliance and Governance

Ensure compliance with industry-specific regulations and governance requirements by configuring auditing with AWS CloudTrail and implementing data encryption and access controls.

## 13. Community and Resources

Leverage the AWS community and resources, including AWS forums, documentation, and whitepapers, to stay updated with best practices and learn from the experiences of others managing large-scale DynamoDB deployments.

## 14. Scaling with AWS Services

Integrate DynamoDB with other AWS services like Lambda, Step Functions, and EventBridge to build scalable serverless applications. These services enable efficient event-driven architectures.

## 15. Real-Time Processing with DynamoDB Streams

Consider using DynamoDB Streams to process real-time data changes and trigger workflows or notifications. This feature can be invaluable for applications requiring real-time insights.

In conclusion, large-scale deployments of Amazon DynamoDB demand careful planning, monitoring, and optimization. By learning from the lessons of successful deployments, you can build robust, high-performance, and cost-effective applications that leverage DynamoDB's capabilities to their fullest extent.

# Chapter 15: The Future of DynamoDB and NoSQL Databases

## Section 15.1: Emerging Trends in NoSQL Technology

NoSQL databases like Amazon DynamoDB continue to evolve in response to changing technology landscapes and the demands of modern applications. In this section, we'll explore some of the emerging trends in NoSQL technology and how they are shaping the future of database management.

### 1. Serverless Databases

Serverless computing has gained significant traction in recent years, and it's influencing the design of NoSQL databases. Serverless databases eliminate the need for users to manage infrastructure, provisioning, and scaling. With services like AWS Aurora Serverless and Amazon DocumentDB, users can focus on application development while the database scales automatically based on workload demand.

### 2. Multi-Model Databases

Traditionally, NoSQL databases have been categorized into document, key-value, column-family, and graph databases. However, multi-model databases are emerging, offering the flexibility to support multiple data models within a single database engine. This trend simplifies data management for applications with diverse data needs.

## 3. Consistency and Transaction Support

NoSQL databases are known for their flexibility and scalability but often sacrifice strong consistency and transaction support. Emerging trends include adding ACID (Atomicity, Consistency, Isolation, Durability) compliance to NoSQL databases, making them suitable for a wider range of use cases, including financial applications.

## 4. Advanced Analytics and Machine Learning Integration

Integrating NoSQL databases with advanced analytics and machine learning platforms is becoming increasingly important. NoSQL databases are being used to store and process large volumes of data, making them a valuable data source for analytics and AI/ML workloads.

## 5. Edge Computing and IoT

The rise of edge computing and the Internet of Things (IoT) has led to increased demand for NoSQL databases that can operate efficiently at the edge. These databases are optimized for low-latency, high-throughput data ingestion and processing in edge locations.

## 6. Time-Series Data

Time-series data, generated by IoT devices, sensors, and applications, is growing exponentially. NoSQL databases are adapting to handle time-series data efficiently. They offer features like data retention policies, automated data aggregation, and time-based indexing for improved query performance.

## 7. Native GraphQL Support

GraphQL is a query language for APIs that allows clients to request only the data they need. Some NoSQL databases are adding native support for GraphQL, simplifying data access and enabling more efficient queries for frontend applications.

## 8. Data Privacy and Compliance

With increasing data privacy concerns and regulations like GDPR and CCPA, NoSQL databases are enhancing their data encryption, access control, and auditing features to help users meet compliance requirements and protect sensitive data.

## 9. Integration with Serverless Architectures

Serverless architectures and NoSQL databases are a natural fit. NoSQL databases are being integrated with serverless compute platforms like AWS Lambda, enabling developers to build scalable, event-driven applications without managing infrastructure.

## 10. Serverless Data Lakes

Serverless data lakes, like AWS Lake Formation, are emerging as a way to centralize and analyze large volumes of data from various sources, including NoSQL databases. This trend simplifies data lake management and analytics.

In summary, NoSQL databases like Amazon DynamoDB are evolving to meet the demands of modern applications. They are adapting to trends such as serverless computing, multi-model support, stronger consistency, advanced analytics, and IoT. As technology continues to advance, NoSQL databases will play a crucial role in enabling scalable and flexible data management solutions.

## Section 15.2: DynamoDB's Roadmap and Future Features

Amazon DynamoDB, a fully managed NoSQL database service, has consistently evolved to meet the needs of developers and businesses. In this section, we'll explore DynamoDB's roadmap and some of the anticipated features and improvements that may shape its future.

### 1. Global Reach

DynamoDB is expected to continue expanding its global footprint, with more regions and availability zones. This expansion will enable users to deploy their applications closer to end-users, improving latency and redundancy.

### 2. Enhanced Query Capabilities

DynamoDB is likely to introduce more advanced querying capabilities, making it even more versatile for a broader range of use cases. This may include support for advanced filtering, aggregation, and analytical queries.

```
# Example of advanced query with filtering

response = dynamodb.query(

TableName='MyTable',

KeyConditionExpression=Key('PartitionKey').eq('123'),

FilterExpression=Attr('Status').eq('Active')

)
```

## 3. Improved Scaling and Auto-Scaling

Scaling DynamoDB may become even more seamless with enhancements in auto-scaling algorithms. Users can expect better tools for predicting and managing capacity requirements as their workloads evolve.

```
# Auto-scaling settings via AWS Management Console

# Users can configure minimum and maximum capacity units.
```

## 4. Data Tiering and Optimization

DynamoDB may introduce features for automatically tiering data based on access patterns. This means frequently accessed data can be stored in high-performance storage, while less frequently accessed data can be moved to cost-effective storage.

```
// Data tiering configuration

const tieringPolicy = {

'FrequentlyAccessed': { ReadCapacity: 5, WriteCapacity: 5 },

'LessFrequentlyAccessed': { ReadCapacity: 1, WriteCapacity: 1 }

};
```

## 5. Deeper Integration with AWS Services

Expect tighter integration between DynamoDB and other AWS services, enabling seamless data flow between various components of your applications. This includes integrations with AWS Lambda, Amazon S3, and Amazon Redshift.

```
# Lambda integration with DynamoDB stream
```

*# Process and transform data in real-time.*

## 6. Enhanced Security Features

Security will remain a priority, and DynamoDB may introduce additional security features such as fine-grained access control, advanced auditing, and anomaly detection for improved protection against security threats.

```
// Fine-grained access control policies

{

"Effect": "Allow",

"Action": "dynamodb:Scan",

"Resource": "arn:aws:dynamodb:us-east-1:123456789012:table/MyTable"

}
```

## 7. Data Lake Integration

DynamoDB may offer improved integration with data lakes, allowing users to seamlessly move data between DynamoDB tables and data lakes like Amazon S3 for advanced analytics and data warehousing.

```
—SQL query to join data from DynamoDB and data lake

SELECT d.*, l.*

FROM DynamoDBTable d

JOIN DataLake l ON d.Key = l.Key;
```

## 8. Support for More Data Types

To accommodate diverse data requirements, DynamoDB may add support for additional data types, including complex data structures like arrays, sets, and nested documents.

```
// Example of a DynamoDB item with nested data
{
"UserID": "12345",
"UserName": "JohnDoe",
"Interests": ["Music", "Travel", "Technology"],
"Address": {
"Street": "123 Main St",
"City": "Anytown",
"ZipCode": "98765"
}
}
```

## 9. Real-time Analytics and Dashboards

Expect improvements in real-time analytics capabilities, making it easier to generate insights from your DynamoDB data. Real-time dashboards may become more accessible for monitoring and visualization.

```
// Real-time dashboard with data from DynamoDB
// Visualize key performance metrics.
```

### 10. Developer-Friendly Tools

DynamoDB's developer tools and SDKs may see updates to enhance developer productivity and streamline application development. These tools may include better debugging support and code generation.

As Amazon DynamoDB continues to evolve, it will remain a crucial component of modern cloud-native applications. Staying up to date with its roadmap and new features will help developers leverage its full potential for building scalable and high-performance applications.

---

## Section 15.3: The Role of AI and Machine Learning

In the rapidly evolving landscape of database technologies, artificial intelligence (AI) and machine learning (ML) are playing an increasingly significant role. DynamoDB, as one of Amazon Web Services' flagship databases, is no exception to this trend. In this section, we'll explore how AI and ML are integrated with DynamoDB and how they contribute to its capabilities and future potential.

### 1. Predictive Analytics

One of the primary applications of AI and ML in DynamoDB is predictive analytics. By analyzing historical data stored in DynamoDB tables, machine learning models can make predictions about future trends, customer behavior, and resource requirements. These predictions can help businesses optimize their operations, plan for capacity needs, and make data-driven decisions.

```
# Example of using SageMaker for predictive analytics
```

*# Train and deploy machine learning models.*

## 2. Personalization

AI and ML enable personalized experiences for users. DynamoDB can store and retrieve user profiles and preferences, while machine learning algorithms can process this data to recommend products, content, or services tailored to each user. Personalization enhances user engagement and satisfaction.

*// Personalized recommendations with DynamoDB and ML*

*// Fetch user preferences and suggest relevant items.*

## 3. Fraud Detection and Security

DynamoDB, when combined with ML, can be a powerful tool for fraud detection and security. ML models can analyze transaction data in real-time, identify anomalies, and trigger alerts or automated responses to potential security threats. This is crucial for protecting sensitive information and maintaining trust.

*# Real-time fraud detection using ML and DynamoDB streams*

*# Monitor transactions and detect suspicious activity.*

## 4. Natural Language Processing (NLP)

NLP is another area where DynamoDB can benefit from AI and ML. Textual data stored in DynamoDB tables can be processed with NLP algorithms to extract insights, sentiment analysis, and entity recognition. This is valuable for applications involving customer reviews, social media data, or text-based interactions.

*# NLP analysis of customer reviews stored in DynamoDB*

*# Extract sentiment and key phrases from text data.*

## 5. Recommendations and Content Generation

AI-driven recommendation engines can help businesses suggest products, services, or content to users. DynamoDB can store historical user interactions, and ML models can generate recommendations based on user behavior, preferences, and trends.

*// Content recommendation system with DynamoDB and ML*

*// Suggest articles, movies, or products to users.*

## 6. Operational Efficiency

AI and ML can optimize operational processes within DynamoDB itself. For example, ML can assist in capacity planning and performance tuning by analyzing usage patterns and recommending adjustments to provisioned throughput or indexing strategies.

*# ML-powered capacity planning for DynamoDB*

*# Analyze historical usage data to optimize resources.*

## 7. Automated Maintenance

Machine learning can be used to automate routine maintenance tasks, such as index optimization, data archival, and backup management. By continuously learning from the database's behavior, ML models can suggest and execute maintenance actions.

*# Automated index optimization with ML insights*

*# Improve query performance based on usage patterns.*

## 8. Data Anomaly Detection

ML models can be trained to detect data anomalies within DynamoDB tables, helping organizations maintain data quality. Whether it's spotting outliers, missing values, or inconsistencies, ML can aid in data cleansing and validation.

*# Data anomaly detection in DynamoDB using ML*

*# Identify and rectify data quality issues.*

## 9. Cost Optimization

AI-driven cost optimization strategies can analyze DynamoDB usage patterns and recommend cost-saving measures. For example, by identifying underutilized resources or suggesting more efficient query patterns.

*# AI-based cost optimization for DynamoDB*

*# Reduce expenses by optimizing resource allocation.*

## 10. Continuous Improvement

As AI and ML technologies advance, DynamoDB is likely to incorporate new features and integrations that facilitate more seamless AI and ML adoption. This includes easier integration with AI platforms, pre-built ML models, and enhanced support for training custom models.

In conclusion, AI and machine learning are integral to the future of DynamoDB. By leveraging these technologies, businesses can unlock new insights, enhance user experiences, improve security, and optimize operations. As the field of AI and ML continues to evolve, DynamoDB's role as a data store and analytics platform will expand, making it even more powerful and versatile for a wide range of applications.

## Section 15.4: DynamoDB in the Context of Big Data

In the era of big data, where organizations deal with massive volumes of data, DynamoDB plays a crucial role in providing scalable and reliable storage solutions. This section delves into the significance of DynamoDB in the context of big data analytics, its integration with other AWS services, and best practices for handling large-scale data.

### 1. Scalability for Big Data

DynamoDB's ability to scale horizontally makes it well-suited for big data applications. As data volumes grow, you can seamlessly increase the provisioned throughput or switch to on-demand mode to handle unpredictable workloads. The automatic sharding of data across multiple partitions ensures that DynamoDB maintains low latency, even with vast datasets.

*# Scaling DynamoDB for big data workloads*

*# Adjust provisioned throughput as data grows.*

### 2. Integration with AWS Analytics Services

To analyze big data stored in DynamoDB, AWS provides several analytics services, including Amazon Athena, Amazon Redshift, and Amazon EMR (Elastic MapReduce). These services allow you to run complex queries, perform data warehousing, and process data with tools like Apache Spark and Hadoop.

*—Querying DynamoDB data with Amazon Athena*

*—Analyze and visualize data stored in DynamoDB tables.*

## 3. DynamoDB Streams for Real-time Processing

DynamoDB Streams enables real-time data processing by capturing changes made to DynamoDB tables. This feature is valuable for applications that require event-driven architectures, real-time analytics, and immediate responses to data changes.

*# Real-time processing with DynamoDB Streams*

*# React to changes in DynamoDB tables in real-time.*

## 4. Data Archiving and Retention

As big data accumulates, it's essential to manage data archiving and retention effectively. DynamoDB's Time to Live (TTL) feature allows you to define a specific expiration time for items, automatically removing outdated data. This feature simplifies data lifecycle management.

// **Implementing data archiving with DynamoDB TTL**

// **Set item expiration to maintain data freshness.**

## 5. Efficient Data Retrieval

To extract meaningful insights from large datasets in DynamoDB, efficient data retrieval is critical. Utilize secondary indexes and proper query optimization techniques to retrieve specific subsets of data efficiently. Pagination and parallel scanning can be employed for retrieving large result sets.

*// Efficient data retrieval from DynamoDB*

*// Use secondary indexes and pagination for large datasets.*

## 6. Data Backup and Recovery

Big data applications require robust data backup and recovery strategies. DynamoDB offers automated and manual backup options, allowing you to create full backups and point-in-time recovery snapshots. These features ensure data durability and facilitate data restoration in case of errors.

*# Data backup and recovery in DynamoDB*

*# Create and restore backups for data protection.*

## 7. Cost Optimization

Optimizing costs when dealing with big data is a top priority. DynamoDB's on-demand pricing mode can be advantageous for sporadic workloads, while provisioned mode allows cost predictability for steady-state workloads. Regularly reviewing and optimizing your data model and indexing can lead to significant cost savings.

*# Cost optimization strategies for DynamoDB*

*# Choose the right pricing mode and optimize data structures.*

## 8. Security and Compliance

Handling big data often involves sensitive information, making security and compliance essential. DynamoDB provides encryption at rest and in transit, fine-grained access control through IAM roles, and integration with AWS CloudTrail for auditing. Adhering to data protection regulations is crucial when dealing with large datasets.

// **Ensuring security and compliance in big data with DynamoDB**

**// Implement encryption, access control, and auditing.**

## 9. Data Quality and Governance

Maintaining data quality in big data scenarios can be challenging. Implement data quality checks, validation rules, and data governance practices to ensure that your data remains accurate and reliable, even at scale.

*# Data quality and governance for big data in DynamoDB*

*# Establish data validation and governance processes.*

## 10. Data Lakes and Data Warehouses

In some big data architectures, data lakes and data warehouses play a crucial role. DynamoDB can seamlessly integrate with these systems, allowing you to extract, transform, and load (ETL) data from DynamoDB into data lakes like Amazon S3 or data warehouses like Amazon Redshift.

*—Data integration from DynamoDB to Amazon Redshift*

*—Perform ETL processes for data warehousing.*

In conclusion, DynamoDB's scalability, real-time capabilities, and integration with AWS analytics services make it a powerful solution for handling big data. By following best practices, optimizing costs, and ensuring data security and quality, you can leverage DynamoDB effectively in the context of big data analytics, enabling your organization to make data-driven decisions and gain valuable insights from vast datasets.

## Section 15.5: Preparing for Future Challenges and Opportunities

As technology and business landscapes continue to evolve, it's essential to prepare for future challenges and opportunities when using DynamoDB and NoSQL databases. This section discusses key considerations and strategies to ensure that your database infrastructure remains adaptive and capable of meeting emerging demands.

### 1. Embrace Serverless Architectures

Serverless computing, powered by services like AWS Lambda, has gained prominence for its flexibility and cost-effectiveness. Consider integrating DynamoDB with serverless functions to create efficient and scalable microservices. This approach allows you to execute code in response to events, reducing the need for traditional server management.

*# Serverless architecture with DynamoDB and AWS Lambda*

*# Execute code in response to DynamoDB table events.*

### 2. Keep Abreast of DynamoDB Updates

AWS regularly updates DynamoDB with new features and improvements. Stay informed about these updates by following AWS announcements, blogs, and documentation. Evaluate how new features can enhance your application's performance, security, and scalability, and consider implementing them as needed.

*# Check for DynamoDB updates and feature releases*

*# Evaluate new features for potential benefits.*

## 3. Leverage Machine Learning and AI

Machine learning (ML) and artificial intelligence (AI) technologies can complement DynamoDB by providing advanced analytics and insights. AWS offers services like Amazon SageMaker for ML model development and integration. Explore ML and AI solutions to extract valuable information from your data and improve decision-making.

*# Integrating machine learning with DynamoDB*

*# Use ML models for data analysis and predictions.*

## 4. Implement Data Governance

As data volumes grow, maintaining data quality and governance becomes increasingly challenging. Establish robust data governance practices, including data lineage, data cataloging, and metadata management. Implement data validation rules and data quality checks to ensure data accuracy and reliability.

*—Data governance practices in DynamoDB*

*—Document data lineage and maintain a data catalog.*

## 5. Plan for Disaster Recovery

Unforeseen events can disrupt database operations. Develop comprehensive disaster recovery plans that include data backup and restoration procedures. Use AWS services like Amazon S3 for backup storage and regularly test your recovery processes to minimize downtime in case of failures.

*# Disaster recovery planning for DynamoDB*

*# Test backup and restoration procedures.*

## 6. Explore Data Lakes and Analytics

Consider augmenting your data infrastructure by incorporating data lakes and advanced analytics tools. Store data from DynamoDB in data lakes like Amazon S3 to enable data exploration and ad-hoc analysis. Leverage AWS analytics services like Amazon Redshift for data warehousing and Amazon QuickSight for interactive dashboards.

*—Integrating DynamoDB data with Amazon Redshift*

*—Enable data warehousing for advanced analytics.*

## 7. Optimize Costs Continuously

Cost optimization is an ongoing process. Regularly review your DynamoDB usage to identify areas where cost savings can be achieved. Adjust your provisioned capacity, use on-demand mode when appropriate, and employ cost monitoring tools like AWS Cost Explorer to manage expenses effectively.

*# Continuous cost optimization strategies for DynamoDB*

*# Monitor costs and make adjustments as needed.*

## 8. Stay Compliant with Regulations

Data protection regulations are continually evolving. Ensure that your data management practices comply with applicable laws and regulations, such as GDPR, HIPAA, or CCPA. Use encryption, access controls, and auditing to maintain data security and compliance.

**// Regulatory compliance in DynamoDB**

**// Implement encryption and access controls as required.**

## 9. Foster a Culture of Innovation

Encourage a culture of innovation within your organization. Empower your teams to explore new technologies and approaches. Create an environment where experimentation is encouraged, allowing you to adapt to changing business needs and technological advancements.

**Innovation Challenge:**

Encourage teams to propose innovative projects leveraging DynamoDB.

## 10. Educate and Upskill

Invest in the education and upskilling of your teams. Provide training on DynamoDB and related AWS services to ensure that your staff is equipped with the knowledge and skills needed to optimize and maintain your database infrastructure effectively.

**Training Program:**

Offer regular training sessions on DynamoDB and cloud best practices.

By addressing these considerations and strategies, you can position your organization to embrace future challenges and opportunities effectively. DynamoDB, when used in conjunction with AWS services and best practices, can be a pivotal component of your evolving technology stack, enabling you to stay competitive and innovative in the ever-changing landscape of data management.

# Chapter 16: Working with Large-Scale Data in DynamoDB

## Section 16.1: Handling Big Data Challenges

When dealing with large-scale data in Amazon DynamoDB, it's essential to address the challenges that come with managing big data efficiently. Big data is characterized by the volume, velocity, variety, and veracity of data. DynamoDB offers several strategies to handle these challenges effectively.

### 1. Data Sharding

One way to manage large datasets is by using data sharding. Sharding involves dividing a large dataset into smaller, more manageable partitions or shards. In DynamoDB, sharding is achieved by using partition keys. Each shard contains a subset of data, and DynamoDB automatically distributes these shards across multiple servers to ensure scalability and performance. By designing your data model with an appropriate partition key, you can distribute the data evenly and avoid hot partitions.

### 2. Adaptive Capacity Scaling

DynamoDB offers adaptive capacity scaling, which allows your tables to automatically adjust their read and write capacity based on the workload. When dealing with large-scale data, workload patterns can vary significantly over time. Adaptive capacity scaling ensures that you don't over-provision resources, saving costs during periods of low traffic and automatically scaling up to handle high traffic without manual intervention.

## 3. Time to Live (TTL)

Managing data retention in large-scale applications can be challenging. DynamoDB provides a Time to Live (TTL) feature that allows you to define a specific expiration time for items in a table. This feature is useful for automatically deleting outdated or irrelevant data, reducing storage costs, and ensuring that your database remains lean and efficient.

## 4. Stream Processing

For real-time data processing and analysis of large-scale data, DynamoDB Streams can be invaluable. DynamoDB Streams capture changes to your data in real time, such as inserts, updates, and deletes, and make these changes available for processing by AWS Lambda or other stream consumers. This feature enables you to react to data changes immediately and build real-time analytics or triggers based on your data.

## 5. Parallel Scans and Queries

When querying or scanning large datasets, you can utilize parallelism to improve performance. DynamoDB allows you to perform parallel scans and queries by dividing the scan or query operation into smaller segments and processing them concurrently. This approach can significantly reduce the time required to retrieve data from large tables.

## 6. Data Compression

Efficient storage is crucial for large-scale data applications. DynamoDB supports data compression, allowing you to store data in a more space-efficient format. By enabling compression, you can reduce storage costs and improve read and write performance, especially when dealing with large volumes of data.

### 7. Monitoring and Optimization

Monitoring the performance and health of your DynamoDB tables is essential for large-scale data management. Use AWS CloudWatch to track key performance metrics, set up alarms for unusual behavior, and optimize your tables accordingly. Regularly reviewing and fine-tuning your data model, partition keys, and indexing strategies can help maintain optimal performance as your data scales.

In summary, handling big data challenges in DynamoDB involves a combination of data modeling, automation, and optimization strategies. By implementing these techniques and leveraging DynamoDB's features, you can effectively manage and process large-scale data while maintaining high availability and performance.

## Section 16.2: Partitioning Strategies for Large Datasets

In Amazon DynamoDB, partitioning is a fundamental concept for distributing and scaling your data. It involves dividing your data into partitions, also known as shards, and distributing them across multiple servers to ensure high availability and performance. When working with large datasets, choosing the right partitioning strategy becomes critical to avoid hot partitions, optimize throughput, and maintain low latency. Here, we will explore various partitioning strategies for handling large datasets effectively.

### 1. Evenly Distributed Partition Keys

To prevent hot partitions, which can lead to unevenly distributed workload and decreased performance, it's crucial to choose partition keys that distribute data evenly. Avoid selecting partition keys with limited variation, such as timestamps that all fall within the same range. Instead, consider using unique identifiers or a combination of attributes that provide a wide distribution of data across partitions.

```
# Example of an evenly distributed partition key in DynamoDB

{

"user_id": "unique_user_id",

"timestamp": "2024-01-28T12:00:00Z"

}
```

## 2. Composite Partition Keys

For large datasets with complex access patterns, consider using composite partition keys that combine multiple attributes. This approach allows you to distribute data effectively and cater to various query requirements.

```
# Example of a composite partition key in DynamoDB

{

"region": "US",

"category": "electronics"

}
```

## 3. Time-Based Partitioning

Time-based partitioning is suitable for scenarios where data is time-sensitive, such as logs or events. You can create separate tables or partitions for different time intervals (e.g., daily, weekly, or monthly), ensuring that older data can be archived or deleted when it expires.

```
# Example of time-based partitioning in DynamoDB
{
"date": "2024-01-28",
"event_id": "unique_event_id"
}
```

## 4. Automatic Sharding with UUIDs

Generating UUIDs (Universally Unique Identifiers) as partition keys can help ensure data distribution. UUIDs are designed to be globally unique, reducing the risk of hot partitions. DynamoDB supports automatic sharding with UUIDs, making it a convenient choice for large datasets.

```
# Example of using UUIDs as partition keys in DynamoDB
{
"uuid": "550e8400-e29b-41d4-a716-446655440000"
}
```

## 5. Global Secondary Indexes (GSI)

When dealing with large datasets and complex querying requirements, leverage Global Secondary Indexes (GSI) to facilitate efficient access patterns. GSIs allow you to define alternative partition and sort keys, enabling diverse queries without impacting the main table's partitioning strategy.

```
# Example of using a Global Secondary Index in DynamoDB

{

"user_id": "unique_user_id",

"order_id": "unique_order_id"

}
```

## 6. Monitoring and Optimization

Regularly monitor the performance of your DynamoDB tables, especially as your dataset grows. Use AWS CloudWatch to track metrics like consumed capacity, throttled requests, and latency. By identifying performance bottlenecks, you can fine-tune your partitioning strategy, adjust provisioned capacity, or implement auto-scaling to optimize the handling of large datasets.

In conclusion, effective partitioning is key to successfully managing and scaling large datasets in DynamoDB. By selecting appropriate partition keys, considering composite keys, and monitoring performance, you can ensure even data distribution, minimize hot partitions, and provide high-performance access to your data, even as it continues to grow.

---

# Section 16.3: Efficient Data Archiving and Retrieval

Managing large-scale data in Amazon DynamoDB not only involves optimizing data access and partitioning but also includes efficiently archiving and retrieving data, especially when historical data needs to be preserved for compliance, analytics, or auditing purposes. In this section, we will explore strategies for efficiently archiving and retrieving data from DynamoDB.

## 1. Time-to-Live (TTL) Expiry

Amazon DynamoDB provides a Time-to-Live (TTL) feature that allows you to set a specific expiration timestamp for items in a table. When an item's TTL expires, DynamoDB automatically removes it from the table. This feature is particularly useful for managing data that has a defined retention period, such as logs or temporary records.

Here's an example of how to enable TTL for an item in a DynamoDB table using the AWS SDK for Python (Boto3):

```
import boto3

# Initialize DynamoDB client

dynamodb = boto3.client('dynamodb')

# Enable TTL for a specific table

table_name = 'MyTable'

ttl_attribute = 'expiry_timestamp' # Name of the TTL attribute

dynamodb.update_time_to_live(

TableName=table_name,

TimeToLiveSpecification={

'AttributeName': ttl_attribute,

'Enabled': True

}

)
```

## 2. Archiving to Amazon S3

For long-term data retention and cost-effective storage, consider archiving historical data to Amazon S3. You can create automated processes or Lambda functions triggered by TTL expirations to move expired items from DynamoDB to S3. By doing so, you retain access to the data while reducing the storage costs in DynamoDB.

Here's a simplified example of archiving data to S3 using Python and Boto3:

```
import boto3

# Initialize DynamoDB and S3 clients

dynamodb = boto3.client('dynamodb')

s3 = boto3.client('s3')

# Define DynamoDB table and S3 bucket names

table_name = 'MyTable'

s3_bucket = 'my-s3-bucket'

# Query DynamoDB for expired items

expired_items = dynamodb.query(

TableName=table_name,

IndexName='TTLIndex', # Assuming you have a TTL-indexed table

KeyConditionExpression='expiry_timestamp < :now',

ExpressionAttributeValues={

':now': {'S': '2024-01-28T12:00:00Z'} # Current timestamp
```

```
}
)['Items']
# Archive expired items to S3
for item in expired_items:
item_id = item['item_id']['S'] # Replace with your primary key
s3_key = f'archived/{item_id}.json'
s3.put_object(Bucket=s3_bucket, Key=s3_key, Body=json.dumps(item))
```

## 3. Querying Archived Data

When you need to access archived data stored in Amazon S3, you can use various querying and analysis tools, such as Amazon Athena, AWS Glue, or Amazon Redshift Spectrum. These services allow you to perform SQL queries on data stored in S3, providing flexibility in retrieving historical information for reporting or analysis.

## 4. Data Lifecycle Management

Implementing a well-defined data lifecycle management policy is essential to ensure that archived data is regularly reviewed, retained as required, and purged when it's no longer needed. AWS services like AWS Data Lifecycle Manager can help automate these processes, ensuring compliance and cost optimization.

Efficient data archiving and retrieval strategies are critical for managing large-scale data in Amazon DynamoDB. Leveraging TTL, archiving to S3, querying archived data using analytical services, and implementing data lifecycle policies can help you strike the right balance between cost-effectiveness and data accessibility.

# Section 16.4: Analyzing Big Data with DynamoDB

Amazon DynamoDB is a powerful NoSQL database for handling large-scale data, but analyzing this data efficiently is equally important. In this section, we'll explore methods for analyzing big data with DynamoDB.

## 1. Exporting Data to Analytical Tools

One common approach for analyzing data stored in DynamoDB is to export it to analytical tools or data warehouses. Amazon offers services like AWS Glue, Amazon Redshift, and Amazon Athena that can query and analyze data stored in DynamoDB.

For example, you can use AWS Glue to extract data from DynamoDB, transform it, and load it into Amazon Redshift for complex analytics. Here's a simplified example using AWS Glue:

```
from awsglue.context import GlueContext

from pyspark.context import SparkContext

# Initialize Spark and Glue contexts

sc = SparkContext()

glueContext = GlueContext(sc)

# Extract data from DynamoDB

dynamodb_df = glueContext.create_dynamic_frame.from_catalog(

database = "your-database-name",

table_name = "your-dynamodb-table-name"
```

```
)
# Transform and load data into Amazon Redshift
glueContext.write_dynamic_frame.from_jdbc_conf(
frame = dynamodb_df,
catalog_connection = "redshift-connection",
connection_options = {"dbtable": "redshift-table-name"},
redshift_tmp_dir = "s3://your-s3-temp-directory/"
)
```

## 2. DynamoDB Streams for Real-Time Analytics

DynamoDB Streams allow you to capture changes made to your DynamoDB tables in real-time. You can use these streams to feed data into real-time analytics pipelines or to trigger Lambda functions for immediate data processing. This is particularly useful when you need to react to changes in your DynamoDB data as they occur.

## 3. On-Demand Data Exports

DynamoDB provides an on-demand data export feature, which allows you to export table data to Amazon S3 in various formats, such as JSON or CSV. This data can then be used for analytics using tools like AWS Glue or directly queried with Amazon Athena. On-demand exports can be scheduled and configured to meet your analytics needs.

## 4. Using PartiQL for Querying

Amazon DynamoDB supports PartiQL, a SQL-compatible query language that allows you to perform complex queries on your data.

You can use PartiQL to query and filter data stored in DynamoDB, making it easier to analyze and extract meaningful insights from your large-scale datasets.

### 5. Cost Optimization

Analyzing big data can be costly, so it's essential to optimize costs. Configure data retention policies to archive or delete data that is no longer needed for analysis. Choose the appropriate analytics services and data storage solutions based on your workload and budget.

Analyzing big data in Amazon DynamoDB requires a combination of export, transformation, and analytics services. Whether you're using AWS Glue, Amazon Redshift, DynamoDB Streams, or PartiQL, understanding the right tools and techniques for your use case is crucial for deriving insights from your large-scale data.

## Section 16.5: Case Studies of Large-Scale Data Management

In this section, we'll explore real-world case studies of organizations successfully managing large-scale data with Amazon DynamoDB. These examples highlight the versatility and effectiveness of DynamoDB in handling massive amounts of data for various use cases.

### 1. Netflix: Scalable User Profiles

Netflix, a global streaming giant, relies on DynamoDB to manage user profiles efficiently. With millions of subscribers worldwide, Netflix uses DynamoDB to store and retrieve user preferences, viewing history, and recommendations. DynamoDB's ability to scale on-demand ensures that Netflix can handle rapid changes in user activity, making it an essential component of their streaming platform.

## 2. Samsung: IoT Data Processing

Samsung utilizes DynamoDB to process and store data from Internet of Things (IoT) devices. From smart TVs to home appliances, Samsung's IoT ecosystem generates massive amounts of data. DynamoDB's scalability and low-latency performance enable Samsung to collect, process, and analyze this data in real-time, improving user experiences and device functionality.

## 3. Lyft: Real-Time Ride Data

Lyft, a prominent ride-sharing company, relies on DynamoDB to manage real-time ride data. DynamoDB efficiently handles the constant stream of ride requests, driver locations, and passenger details. This real-time data processing ensures that passengers are matched with drivers swiftly and accurately, contributing to Lyft's success in the competitive ride-sharing market.

## 4. Airbnb: Managing User Bookings

Airbnb, a leading online marketplace for lodging and travel experiences, uses DynamoDB to manage user bookings and property listings. DynamoDB's flexible schema and scalability allow Airbnb to accommodate a vast and diverse range of properties and bookings globally. It ensures that users can search, book, and manage their accommodations seamlessly.

## 5. Capital One: Fraud Detection

Capital One, a major financial institution, employs DynamoDB for fraud detection and prevention. DynamoDB stores transaction data from millions of customers, allowing Capital One's algorithms to analyze transactions in real-time for suspicious activity. This helps protect customers from fraudulent charges and ensures the security of their financial data.

## 6. iFood: Food Delivery at Scale

iFood, a popular food delivery platform in Latin America, relies on DynamoDB to manage food orders, restaurant listings, and delivery logistics. DynamoDB's ability to handle high traffic during peak meal times ensures that customers can place orders efficiently, restaurants can manage their menus, and drivers can deliver food promptly.

These case studies demonstrate the versatility of Amazon DynamoDB in managing large-scale data across various industries. Whether it's streaming services, IoT data, ride-sharing, travel bookings, financial transactions, or food delivery, DynamoDB's scalability, flexibility, and real-time capabilities make it a go-to choice for organizations dealing with massive data volumes and demanding workloads.

# Chapter 17: Integrations and Ecosystem

## Section 17.1: Connecting DynamoDB with Other AWS Services

In this section, we will explore the integration possibilities of Amazon DynamoDB with other AWS services. DynamoDB's compatibility with the AWS ecosystem allows you to build robust and scalable applications by leveraging various complementary services.

Amazon Web Services offers a wide array of tools and services that can enhance your DynamoDB-based applications, providing features like data analytics, serverless computing, real-time event processing, and more. Let's delve into some of the key AWS services that can seamlessly integrate with DynamoDB.

### 1. AWS Lambda

AWS Lambda allows you to execute code in response to events. You can trigger Lambda functions based on changes in your DynamoDB tables. For example, you can invoke a Lambda function when a new item is added to a DynamoDB table, enabling you to perform real-time processing or data transformation.

Here's a simple example of how to set up a Lambda function triggered by DynamoDB events using the AWS SDK for JavaScript:

```
const AWS = require('aws-sdk');

exports.handler = async (event) => {

const dynamoDB = new AWS.DynamoDB.DocumentClient();
```

```
for (const record of event.Records) {
if (record.eventName === 'INSERT') {
const newItem = AWS.DynamoDB.Converter.unmarshall(record.dynamodb.NewImage);
// Your custom logic here
console.log('New item added:', newItem);
}
}
return 'Lambda function executed successfully!';
};
```

## 2. Amazon S3

Amazon S3 (Simple Storage Service) is a highly scalable object storage service that can be used to store and retrieve data generated or processed by DynamoDB. You can use S3 to archive historical data, store backups, or host static assets for your web applications.

## 3. Amazon Kinesis

Amazon Kinesis provides real-time streaming data services. You can use Kinesis Data Streams to capture and process data from various sources, including DynamoDB Streams. This allows you to build real-time analytics, dashboards, and applications that react to changes in your DynamoDB tables.

### 4. AWS Step Functions

AWS Step Functions enables you to build serverless workflows by orchestrating AWS services, including DynamoDB. You can create workflows that perform complex operations involving DynamoDB, Lambda, S3, and other services.

### 5. Amazon Redshift

Amazon Redshift is a fully managed data warehousing service that can be used to analyze large volumes of data, including data stored in DynamoDB. You can use Redshift Spectrum to query data directly from S3, which can be populated with data from DynamoDB.

These are just a few examples of how DynamoDB can be integrated with other AWS services to create powerful and flexible applications. By harnessing the capabilities of the AWS ecosystem, you can extend the functionality of your DynamoDB-based solutions and address a wide range of use cases efficiently.

---

## Section 17.2: Third-Party Tools and Extensions for DynamoDB

In addition to AWS services, there are various third-party tools and extensions available that can further enhance your experience with Amazon DynamoDB. These tools provide additional functionalities, monitoring capabilities, and integrations that cater to specific use cases and preferences.

### 1. DynamoDB GUI Clients

Several third-party GUI clients simplify working with DynamoDB, providing a user-friendly interface for managing tables, items, and queries. Examples include NoSQL Workbench for Amazon

DynamoDB (official AWS tool) and DynamoDB Accelerator (DAX) Console.

## 2. Data Migration Tools

For migrating data in and out of DynamoDB, you can use third-party tools like AWS Data Pipeline, AWS Glue, or open-source solutions like Dynaomodb-Bee.

## 3. Monitoring and Performance Tools

To monitor and optimize DynamoDB performance, consider tools like Dynatrace, New Relic, and Datadog. These tools offer advanced analytics, alerting, and visualization features.

## 4. Document and Object Mappers

If you prefer working with DynamoDB in a more object-oriented or document-based way, libraries like the AWS SDK for JavaScript (DocumentClient), DynamoDBMapper for Java, or PynamoDB for Python provide convenient abstractions.

## 5. Framework Integrations

Popular web frameworks like Spring Boot for Java and Serverless Framework[1] for Node.js, Python, and more have plugins and integrations for DynamoDB. These make it easier to develop serverless applications using DynamoDB as a data store.

1. https://www.serverless.com/

## 6. Backup and Restore Solutions

Third-party solutions like DynamoDB Backup[2] offer automated backup and restore capabilities, which can complement DynamoDB's built-in backup features.

## 7. Caching with Redis

When you need to implement caching for DynamoDB queries, you can integrate Amazon ElastiCache for Redis to speed up read-heavy workloads and reduce the load on DynamoDB.

## 8. Advanced Querying

Tools like Amazon Athena and Amazon Quicksight can be used to perform complex ad-hoc queries and visualize data stored in DynamoDB.

## 9. Local Development

For local development and testing, you can use tools like DynamoDB Local or DynamoDB Docker to simulate DynamoDB on your development machine.

These third-party tools and extensions provide flexibility and additional features to enhance your DynamoDB development and operations. Depending on your specific requirements and workflows, you can leverage these tools to streamline your interactions with DynamoDB and create more efficient applications.

# Section 17.3: Building a DevOps Pipeline

Building a DevOps pipeline for Amazon DynamoDB involves automating various stages of development, testing, deployment, and

2. https://www.dynamodbbackup.com/

monitoring. This approach ensures that changes to your DynamoDB infrastructure and applications are managed efficiently, reducing the risk of errors and speeding up the development lifecycle. Here, we'll explore the key components and practices for setting up a DevOps pipeline for DynamoDB.

## 1. Infrastructure as Code (IAC)

Start by defining your DynamoDB infrastructure using Infrastructure as Code (IAC) tools like AWS CloudFormation or AWS CDK (Cloud Development Kit). This allows you to version-control your DynamoDB tables, streams, and other resources. You can use code to create, modify, and delete resources consistently, making it easy to replicate environments across development, testing, and production.

Here's an example of using AWS CDK to define a DynamoDB table:

```
import * as cdk from 'aws-cdk-lib';

import * as dynamodb from 'aws-cdk-lib/aws-dynamodb';

const app = new cdk.App();

const stack = new cdk.Stack(app, 'DynamoDBStack');

const table = new dynamodb.Table(stack, 'MyTable', {

partitionKey: { name: 'userID', type: dynamodb.AttributeType.STRING },

readCapacity: 5,

writeCapacity: 5,

});
```

## 2. Automated Testing

Implement automated tests for your DynamoDB applications to validate functionality and performance. Unit tests, integration tests, and load tests can help identify issues early in the development cycle. You can use testing frameworks and AWS SDKs to create test suites that interact with DynamoDB tables, ensuring that your application behaves as expected.

## 3. Continuous Integration (CI)

Set up a CI system (e.g., AWS CodePipeline, Jenkins, or GitHub Actions) to automate the build and testing of your DynamoDB-backed applications. Whenever code changes are pushed to your version control system, the CI pipeline triggers builds and runs tests automatically. This ensures that code is validated before it's merged into the main branch.

## 4. Version Control and Git Flow

Use version control systems like Git and follow a branching strategy like Git Flow to manage changes to your DynamoDB infrastructure and application code. This approach allows for collaboration among team members and ensures that changes are tracked, reviewed, and merged systematically.

## 5. Deployment Automation

Automate deployments of your DynamoDB-backed applications using tools like AWS Elastic Beanstalk, AWS Lambda, or AWS Fargate. You can define deployment pipelines that promote changes from one environment (e.g., staging) to another (e.g., production) in a controlled and repeatable manner.

## 6. Monitoring and Alerting

Implement robust monitoring and alerting for your DynamoDB tables and applications. AWS CloudWatch, along with custom metrics and alarms, can help you track table performance, monitor resource utilization, and detect anomalies. Set up notifications to alert your team in case of issues.

## 7. Rollback Mechanism

Plan for rollback procedures in case of deployment failures or unexpected issues. Having a well-defined rollback process ensures that you can quickly revert to a previous working state of your DynamoDB infrastructure and applications.

## 8. Security and Compliance

Incorporate security and compliance checks into your DevOps pipeline. Implement AWS Identity and Access Management (IAM) policies, AWS Config rules, and AWS Trusted Advisor checks to ensure that your DynamoDB resources adhere to security best practices and compliance standards.

## 9. Continuous Improvement

Continuously monitor and assess your DevOps pipeline for DynamoDB. Collect feedback from your team, identify bottlenecks or areas for improvement, and iteratively enhance your pipeline to streamline operations and reduce manual intervention.

By following these practices and integrating DynamoDB into your DevOps pipeline, you can ensure that your applications are developed, deployed, and operated efficiently and securely while minimizing downtime and errors.

# Section 17.4: Data Migration Tools and Techniques

In this section, we will explore data migration tools and techniques for Amazon DynamoDB. Data migration is a critical aspect of database management, especially when transitioning between environments or platforms. Whether you are moving data into DynamoDB for the first time or migrating it out to another storage solution, having a solid understanding of the available tools and best practices is essential.

## Understanding Data Migration

Data migration involves transferring data from one location or format to another. In the context of DynamoDB, this can include:

- **Importing Data:** Bringing data into DynamoDB from various sources, such as existing databases, CSV files, or data lakes.
- **Exporting Data:** Extracting data from DynamoDB to perform analytics, backup, or to move it to another data store.
- **Schema Transformation:** Converting the data schema to match the requirements of DynamoDB.

## AWS Data Pipeline

AWS Data Pipeline is a web service provided by Amazon Web Services for orchestrating and automating the movement and transformation of data. It can be used for data migration tasks involving DynamoDB. You can create data pipelines that move data into or out of DynamoDB tables.

Here's an example of creating a data pipeline to import data into DynamoDB:

```
{
"objects": [
{
"id": "MyImportPipeline",
"name": "MyImportPipeline",
"fields": [
{
"key": "myDynamoDBInputData",
"stringValue": "DDBImportTableData"
}
]
}
]
}
```

## AWS Database Migration Service (DMS)

AWS Database Migration Service (DMS) is another tool provided by AWS for migrating data from various sources to DynamoDB and vice versa. DMS supports both one-time data migrations and continuous data replication.

To migrate data to DynamoDB using AWS DMS, you would typically follow these steps:

1. Create a replication instance and endpoints for source and target databases.
2. Create a replication instance and endpoints for source and target databases.
3. Create a replication instance and endpoints for source and target databases.
4. Create a replication instance and endpoints for source and target databases.
5. Create a replication instance and endpoints for source and target databases.
6. Create a replication instance and endpoints for source and target databases.
7. Create a replication instance and endpoints for source and target databases.
8. Create a replication instance and endpoints for source and target databases.
9. Create a replication instance and endpoints for source and target databases.
10. Create a replication instance and endpoints for source and target databases.
11. Create a replication instance and endpoints for source and target databases.
12. Create a replication instance and endpoints for source and target databases.
13. Create a replication instance and endpoints for source and target databases.
14. Create a replication instance and endpoints for source and

target databases.

15. Create a replication instance and endpoints for source and target databases.
16. Create a replication instance and endpoints for source and target databases.
17. Create a replication instance and endpoints for source and target databases.
18. Create a replication instance and endpoints for source and target databases.
19. Create a replication instance and endpoints for source and target databases.
20. Create a replication instance and endpoints for source and target databases.
21. Create a replication instance and endpoints for source and target databases.
22. Create a replication instance and endpoints for source and target databases.
23. Create a replication instance and endpoints for source and target databases.
24. Create a replication instance and endpoints for source and target databases.
25. Create a replication instance and endpoints for source and target databases.
26. Create a replication instance and endpoints for source and target databases.
27. Create a replication instance and endpoints for source and target databases.
28. Create a replication instance and endpoints for source and target databases.
29. Create a replication instance and endpoints for source and target databases.
30. Create a replication instance and endpoints for source and

target databases.

31. Create a replication instance and endpoints for source and target databases.
32. Create a replication instance and endpoints for source and target databases.
33. Create a replication instance and endpoints for source and target databases.
34. Create a replication instance and endpoints for source and target databases.
35. Create a replication instance and endpoints for source and target databases.
36. Create a replication instance and endpoints for source and target databases.
37. Create a replication instance and endpoints for source and target databases.
38. Create a replication instance and endpoints for source and target databases.
39. Create a replication instance and endpoints for source and target databases.
40. Create a replication instance and endpoints for source and target databases.
41. Create a replication instance and endpoints for source and target databases.
42. Create a replication instance and endpoints for source and target databases.
43. Create a replication instance and endpoints for source and target databases.
44. Create a replication instance and endpoints for source and target databases.
45. Create a replication instance and endpoints for source and target databases.

## Section 17.5: Building a Robust Ecosystem Around DynamoDB

In this section, we will explore how to build a robust ecosystem around Amazon DynamoDB by integrating it with other AWS services and third-party tools. Creating a well-connected and versatile ecosystem can enhance the capabilities and efficiency of your DynamoDB-based applications.

### Integrating with AWS Lambda

AWS Lambda is a serverless computing service that allows you to run code in response to events without managing servers. Integrating DynamoDB with Lambda can enable real-time processing and automation. For example, you can trigger a Lambda function whenever data is added or modified in a DynamoDB table. This is achieved through DynamoDB Streams, which capture and stream database activity to Lambda functions for processing.

Here's a basic example of setting up a Lambda function to process DynamoDB Streams:

```
import boto3

def lambda_handler(event, context):

for record in event['Records']:

# Process the DynamoDB record here

print(record)
```

### Building a DevOps Pipeline

To ensure a smooth and efficient development and deployment process, consider building a DevOps pipeline around DynamoDB.

AWS offers services like AWS CodePipeline and AWS CodeBuild that can automate the build, test, and deployment of your DynamoDB-based applications. This helps in maintaining consistency and reduces the risk of errors.

A simplified example of a CodePipeline configuration for DynamoDB could include source code from a repository (e.g., AWS CodeCommit), build and test stages, and deployment to AWS resources.

## Data Migration Tools and Techniques

In Section 17.4, we discussed data migration tools such as AWS Data Pipeline and AWS Database Migration Service (DMS). Building a robust ecosystem often involves the seamless transfer of data between different storage solutions and services. Leveraging these tools, you can design data pipelines that move data in and out of DynamoDB, ensuring data availability and consistency across your ecosystem.

## Third-Party Tools and Extensions

The AWS ecosystem is extensive, and there are numerous third-party tools and extensions available that can enhance DynamoDB's functionality. For instance, tools like Dynobase[3] provide a user-friendly GUI for DynamoDB development and debugging. Additionally, you can explore libraries and frameworks that simplify DynamoDB integration within your applications.

## Data Migration Tools and Techniques

In Section 17.4, we discussed data migration tools such as AWS Data Pipeline and AWS Database Migration Service (DMS). Building a robust ecosystem often involves the seamless transfer of data between

3. https://dynobase.dev/

different storage solutions and services. Leveraging these tools, you can design data pipelines that move data in and out of DynamoDB, ensuring data availability and consistency across your ecosystem.

## Third-Party Tools and Extensions

The AWS ecosystem is extensive, and there are numerous third-party tools and extensions available that can enhance DynamoDB's functionality. For instance, tools like Dynobase[4] provide a user-friendly GUI for DynamoDB development and debugging. Additionally, you can explore libraries and frameworks that simplify DynamoDB integration within your applications.

## Data Migration Tools and Techniques

In Section 17.4, we discussed data migration tools such as AWS Data Pipeline and AWS Database Migration Service (DMS). Building a robust ecosystem often involves the seamless transfer of data between different storage solutions and services. Leveraging these tools, you can design data pipelines that move data in and out of DynamoDB, ensuring data availability and consistency across your ecosystem.

## Third-Party Tools and Extensions

The AWS ecosystem is extensive, and there are numerous third-party tools and extensions available that can enhance DynamoDB's functionality. For instance, tools like Dynobase[5] provide a user-friendly GUI for DynamoDB development and debugging. Additionally, you can explore libraries and frameworks that simplify DynamoDB integration within your applications.

4. https://dynobase.dev/

5. https://dynobase.dev/

## Monitoring and Logging

To maintain the health and performance of your DynamoDB-based applications, it's crucial to implement monitoring and logging solutions. AWS offers services like Amazon CloudWatch for monitoring and AWS CloudTrail for logging and auditing. Configuring these services allows you to track metrics, set alarms, and gain insights into the behavior of your DynamoDB tables.

## Continuous Integration and Continuous Deployment (CI/CD)

Implementing CI/CD practices in your DynamoDB ecosystem can streamline the development process and improve code quality. Services like AWS CodePipeline, AWS CodeBuild, and AWS CodeDeploy can be integrated to automate testing and deployment workflows. This ensures that changes are thoroughly tested before being deployed to production.

In summary, building a robust ecosystem around Amazon DynamoDB involves integrating it with other AWS services, third-party tools, and implementing best practices for monitoring, logging, and continuous integration. These elements collectively contribute to the reliability, scalability, and efficiency of your DynamoDB-based

# Chapter 18: DynamoDB for Mobile and Web Applications

## Section 18.1: Designing Responsive Applications with DynamoDB

Designing responsive applications with Amazon DynamoDB requires a strategic approach to ensure that the database architecture aligns with the dynamic needs of web and mobile applications. In this section, we discuss best practices and strategies for leveraging DynamoDB in a way that optimizes responsiveness and user experience.

### 1. Understanding Application Requirements

Begin by thoroughly understanding the data access patterns of your application. Identify how frequently data will be read versus written, the types of queries you'll need to support, and the expected volume of traffic. This understanding will guide your decisions on table design, indexing, and capacity planning.

### 2. Table Design

Optimize your DynamoDB table design to cater to your application's access patterns. Use composite keys where appropriate to enable efficient querying. Remember that DynamoDB is schema-less for the most part, which gives you flexibility in storing varied data types.

### 3. Efficient Indexing

Make use of DynamoDB's primary indexes and secondary indexes (Global Secondary Indexes and Local Secondary Indexes) to speed up query times. Indexes should be created based on common query patterns in your application to ensure fast and efficient data retrieval.

### 4. Auto Scaling

Leverage DynamoDB's auto-scaling feature to automatically adjust the read and write capacity of your tables. Auto scaling helps in managing sudden traffic spikes and reduces the need for manual capacity planning, ensuring a responsive application experience.

### 5. Caching with DAX

For read-intensive applications, consider implementing DynamoDB Accelerator (DAX), an in-memory cache. DAX can dramatically speed up read performance, which is particularly beneficial for latency-sensitive mobile and web applications.

### 6. Batch Operations

Use batch operations (BatchGetItem and BatchWriteItem) to retrieve or write multiple items in a single request. This reduces the number of network calls to DynamoDB, thereby improving application performance.

### 7. Data Consistency

Understand the consistency model of DynamoDB. By default, DynamoDB provides eventual consistency, but you can opt for strong consistency for read operations where needed. Choose the right consistency model based on your application requirements.

### 8. Connection Management

Properly manage connections to DynamoDB from your application. Utilize the AWS SDKs which efficiently handle connection pooling and retries. This is crucial for maintaining the responsiveness of your application under various network conditions.

## 9. Handling Large Items

DynamoDB has a size limit for items (400 KB). For larger data, consider storing the actual data in Amazon S3 and keeping a reference to it in DynamoDB. This approach is efficient for handling large blobs like images or videos in your web or mobile applications.

## 10. Monitoring and Logging

Implement monitoring and logging for your DynamoDB usage using Amazon CloudWatch. Monitoring key metrics such as read/write throughput, latency, and error rates will help you keep track of your application's performance and troubleshoot issues.

## 11. Security

Ensure that your application's interaction with DynamoDB is secure. Use AWS Identity and Access Management (IAM) to control access to your DynamoDB resources. Implement fine-grained access control for sensitive data.

## 12. Global Tables for Multi-Region Applications

If your application serves a global user base, consider using DynamoDB Global Tables. Global Tables provide multi-region, fully replicated tables which are ideal for applications that require fast, local access to data for users around the world.

## 13. Time to Live (TTL) for Data Management

Implement TTL to automatically delete items that are no longer needed. This feature is useful for session data, temporary data, or any data that has a natural expiration time.

## 14. Utilizing Streams

Consider using DynamoDB Streams to capture changes in your tables. Streams can trigger AWS Lambda functions for real-time processing, which can be used for notifications, aggregations, or other real-time features in your application.

## 15. Continuous Backup and Point-in-Time Recovery

Enable continuous backup and point-in-time recovery for your DynamoDB tables. This ensures that you can quickly restore your data to any point in time in case of accidental writes or deletes.

## 16. Query Pagination

Implement query pagination in your application. Pagination is essential for handling large datasets and providing a smooth user experience in your web or mobile applications.

## 17. DynamoDB Local for Development

Use DynamoDB Local for local development and testing. It simulates DynamoDB in your development environment, allowing you to develop and test without accessing the actual AWS environment.

## 18. Optimizing Costs

Regularly review your DynamoDB usage and optimize costs. Analyze your read/write capacity modes, reserved capacity, and data storage requirements. Optimize your usage patterns to reduce costs without compromising application performance.

By adhering to these best practices and strategies, you can build responsive, efficient, and scalable mobile and web applications powered by Amazon DynamoDB. Each aspect, from table design to global deployment, plays a crucial role in ensuring that your application can handle the demands of modern web and mobile users.

---

# Section 18.2: Managing User Sessions and State

When developing web and mobile applications, managing user sessions and state effectively is crucial for maintaining a seamless user experience. Amazon DynamoDB, with its high availability and scalability, offers a robust solution for managing session data. In this section, we discuss strategies and best practices for using DynamoDB to handle user sessions and application state.

## 1. Designing Session Management

When designing a session management system with DynamoDB, consider the data structure of your session items. Typically, a session item should contain a unique session identifier, user identifiers, timestamps, and any relevant session data such as user preferences or temporary data.

## 2. Session Table Structure

Create a dedicated DynamoDB table for storing session data. The primary key should be the session identifier, and you can use additional attributes for user information, session start and end times, and any other relevant data.

## 3. Session Timeout and Expiration

Implement session timeout and expiration using DynamoDB's Time to Live (TTL) feature. This automatically deletes sessions that have expired, helping to manage storage costs and maintain data cleanliness.

## 4. Handling Concurrent Sessions

In applications where users might have multiple concurrent sessions (e.g., logged in from multiple devices), structure your session management logic to handle these cases. You might need to track and manage multiple session tokens per user.

## 5. Security Considerations

Ensure that session data is secured. Use fine-grained IAM policies to control access to the session data in DynamoDB. Also, consider encrypting sensitive session data both in transit and at rest.

## 6. Session Data Caching

For frequently accessed session data, consider implementing caching to reduce read load on the DynamoDB table. DynamoDB Accelerator (DAX) is an in-memory cache that can be used for this purpose.

## 7. Scalability

Take advantage of DynamoDB's scalability to handle a large number of sessions. Monitor your read and write throughput and utilize auto-scaling to adjust capacity as needed.

## 8. Integration with Authentication Services

Integrate your session management system with authentication services like Amazon Cognito. This provides a seamless flow for user authentication, session token generation, and session management.

## 9. Session Data Serialization

When storing session data, serialize the data into a format suitable for storage in DynamoDB. Common formats include JSON or XML. When reading the session data, deserialize it back into a usable format for your application.

## 10. State Management for Serverless Applications

In serverless architectures, state management can be challenging due to the stateless nature of services like AWS Lambda. Use DynamoDB to persist state information across function invocations for a consistent user experience.

## 11. Global Session Management

For applications with a global user base, consider using DynamoDB Global Tables to replicate session data across multiple AWS regions. This reduces latency and improves the responsiveness of your application for users worldwide.

## 12. Monitoring and Analytics

Implement monitoring to track the usage and performance of your session management system. Use tools like Amazon CloudWatch to monitor read/write operations, latency, and error rates. This data can be invaluable for troubleshooting and optimizing performance.

## 13. Cleanup Strategies

Regularly review and clean up old or unused session data. This helps in managing storage costs and ensures that your session management system remains efficient.

## 14. Handling Session Hijacking

Implement security measures to prevent session hijacking. Techniques include validating the user's IP address or user agent string, using HTTPS for all communications, and implementing robust token generation and validation methods.

## 15. Updating Session Data

Design your application logic to handle updates to session data efficiently. Minimize write operations to DynamoDB by batching updates or only writing changes to the database.

## 16. User Logout and Session Invalidations

Implement logic for user logout and session invalidation. When a user logs out, ensure that their session is immediately invalidated and removed from DynamoDB.

### 17. Load Testing

Conduct load testing on your session management system to ensure that it can handle the expected number of simultaneous users and sessions.

By following these guidelines, you can create an efficient and scalable session management system for your web and mobile applications using Amazon DynamoDB. Proper session and state management are key to providing a secure and seamless user experience.

## Section 18.3: Real-Time Data Synchronization

Real-time data synchronization is a critical aspect of modern web and mobile applications, ensuring that users have the most current information regardless of their device or location. Amazon DynamoDB, known for its high availability and scalability, can be effectively utilized to achieve real-time data synchronization across various platforms.

### 1. Understanding Data Synchronization

Data synchronization involves keeping data consistent and up-to-date across different systems or devices. In the context of web and mobile applications, this means ensuring that any data change is quickly reflected across all user interfaces and sessions.

### 2. DynamoDB Streams for Data Propagation

DynamoDB Streams is a powerful feature for capturing changes to items in your DynamoDB tables. It can be used to trigger real-time synchronization processes. For example, when an item is updated in a table, the change can be captured by a DynamoDB Stream and processed to update the application state across all platforms.

## 3. Integrating with AWS Lambda

AWS Lambda can be used in conjunction with DynamoDB Streams to process and propagate data changes. Lambda functions can be triggered by stream events, enabling you to execute custom synchronization logic, such as updating cache stores or sending notifications to other systems or services.

## 4. Managing Conflict Resolution

In any data synchronization process, conflict resolution is a key consideration. Implement logic to handle conflicts that might arise when the same data is updated simultaneously from different sources. Techniques such as 'last writer wins' or more complex custom resolution logic can be employed.

## 5. Leveraging Global Tables

For applications that require data synchronization across different geographical regions, DynamoDB Global Tables can be used. They provide automatic multi-region replication, which helps in keeping data synchronized across global AWS regions.

## 6. Caching for Performance

Implement caching strategies to enhance performance. DynamoDB Accelerator (DAX) can be particularly useful for read-heavy applications, as it provides in-memory caching to reduce response times and lighten loads on your DynamoDB tables.

## 7. Change Data Capture (CDC)

Change Data Capture techniques can be used to capture and track data changes. DynamoDB Streams can serve as a CDC mechanism, allowing applications to respond to data changes in real-time.

## 8. Event-Driven Architecture

Adopt an event-driven architecture for your application to facilitate real-time data synchronization. This approach, combined with DynamoDB Streams and AWS Lambda, can create a responsive and dynamic user experience.

## 9. Timestamps and Versioning

Use timestamps and versioning in your data records to track changes and synchronize data accurately. This helps in determining the order of updates and resolving conflicts in a multi-user, multi-device environment.

## 10. User Experience Considerations

Design the user experience to gracefully handle data synchronization. Provide visual indicators or notifications when data is being updated or when the user is viewing stale data.

## 11. Network Connectivity Handling

In mobile applications, handle scenarios where network connectivity is intermittent. Implement local data caching and sync processes that activate when the device reconnects to the network.

## 12. Scalability

Ensure your data synchronization strategy is scalable. As your user base grows, your system should be able to handle increased synchronization demands without degradation in performance.

## 13. Security

Implement robust security measures to protect data during synchronization. Use encryption for data in transit and ensure that your AWS Lambda functions and other integration points follow best security practices.

## 14. Monitoring and Alerts

Use AWS monitoring tools like Amazon CloudWatch to monitor the health and performance of your synchronization processes. Set up alerts for any anomalies or failures in the system.

## 15. Testing

Thoroughly test your data synchronization logic under various scenarios, including conflicting updates, network failures, and high-load conditions. Ensure that your system behaves reliably and consistently.

## 16. Documentation and Best Practices

Maintain comprehensive documentation of your data synchronization strategy and architecture. Document best practices, conflict resolution policies, and any edge cases that your application handles.

### 17. Continuous Improvement

Continuously monitor, analyze, and improve your data synchronization processes. Stay updated with the latest AWS features and enhancements that can benefit your synchronization strategy.

By carefully planning and implementing these strategies, you can ensure robust and efficient real-time data synchronization for your DynamoDB-backed applications, providing a seamless and up-to-date user experience.

## Section 18.4: Offline Support and Data Persistence

In the development of mobile and web applications, providing offline support and ensuring data persistence are crucial for enhancing user experience and reliability. Amazon DynamoDB, when integrated with the right tools and strategies, can effectively support offline scenarios in your applications.

### 1. Understanding Offline Support

Offline support refers to the ability of an application to function without a network connection. This involves storing data locally and synchronizing it with the server once the connection is reestablished.

### 2. Local Data Storage

Implement local data storage in your application. For mobile applications, this could mean using SQLite or Realm DB for storing data locally. Web applications can leverage IndexedDB, LocalStorage, or SessionStorage for this purpose.

## 3. Data Synchronization

Develop a data synchronization mechanism that syncs local data with DynamoDB when the application goes back online. This requires conflict resolution strategies to handle cases where the same data has been modified both locally and on the server.

## 4. Caching Strategies

Implement caching strategies to store frequently accessed data. This reduces the need for network requests and allows the application to display data and function while offline.

## 5. Leveraging AWS AppSync

Consider using AWS AppSync, a managed service that makes it easy to develop applications with offline support. AppSync automatically handles data synchronization and conflict resolution with DynamoDB.

## 6. Background Data Sync

Implement background data synchronization processes in your application. This ensures that local changes are periodically synced to DynamoDB, reducing the likelihood of data loss and conflicts.

## 7. Conflict Resolution Techniques

Employ conflict resolution techniques such as 'last writer wins', version checks, or custom logic to handle synchronization conflicts when the application comes back online.

## 8. User Experience during Offline Mode

Design your application's user interface to inform users when they are in offline mode. Provide feedback on data sync status and allow users to manually trigger synchronization.

## 9. Testing Offline Scenarios

Thoroughly test your application in offline scenarios to ensure data integrity and synchronization work as expected. Simulate various network conditions and offline durations to validate the application's behavior.

## 10. Data Compression

For mobile applications, consider compressing data stored locally to save storage space. Compression is especially important when dealing with large datasets or images.

## 11. Security Considerations

Ensure that locally stored data is secure. Implement encryption for sensitive data and follow best practices for data access and authorization, especially in shared or public devices.

## 12. Managing Local Storage Limits

Be aware of and manage the limits of local storage on different browsers and devices. Implement logic to handle scenarios where the available local storage is insufficient.

## 13. Notifications and Background Tasks

In mobile applications, utilize background tasks and notifications to inform users of important updates or the need to sync data. This can be critical for ensuring that data is not outdated or lost.

## 14. Offline Analytics

Implement offline analytics to track user behavior even when the application is not connected to the internet. This data can be synced and analyzed once the application goes online.

## 15. Progressive Web Apps (PWAs)

For web applications, consider developing a Progressive Web App (PWA). PWAs can provide a native-like experience, including offline support, by leveraging service workers for background syncing and caching.

## 16. Data Partitioning

Partition data logically to optimize for offline usage. Store only necessary data locally to ensure quick access and minimize storage usage.

## 17. Handling Large Data Sets

For applications dealing with large data sets, implement paging or incremental loading techniques. This ensures that only a subset of data is loaded at a time, which is particularly important in offline scenarios.

By incorporating these practices, you can enhance your DynamoDB-powered application with robust offline support and data persistence, providing a seamless and reliable user experience even without a consistent network connection.

## Section 18.5: Case Studies: Successful Mobile and Web Apps

In this section, we delve into a series of case studies focusing on successful mobile and web applications that have effectively utilized Amazon DynamoDB as a part of their technology stack. These case studies showcase diverse applications, each highlighting different aspects of DynamoDB's capabilities.

### 1. E-commerce Platform

An e-commerce giant leveraged DynamoDB to manage their vast inventory and handle high volumes of user transactions. DynamoDB's ability to scale quickly was crucial during peak shopping periods like Black Friday, ensuring smooth and responsive user experiences.

### 2. Social Media App

A popular social media application used DynamoDB for storing user profiles, posts, and interactions. The low latency and high throughput of DynamoDB enabled the app to deliver real-time updates and notifications to a global user base.

### 3. Online Gaming Platform

An online gaming platform utilized DynamoDB for player data management and real-time game state tracking. DynamoDB's fast read and write capabilities were essential for maintaining real-time leaderboard updates and player matchmaking.

## 4. IoT Device Management

A company specializing in IoT devices used DynamoDB to store and process large streams of data from various sensors and devices. The seamless integration with AWS IoT services and the ability to handle large volumes of data made DynamoDB an ideal choice.

## 5. Content Management System

A content management system (CMS) for a news portal used DynamoDB to store and retrieve articles, user comments, and metadata. The CMS benefited from DynamoDB's scalability and managed database services, reducing the overhead of database administration.

## 6. Mobile Health Application

A health tracking mobile application used DynamoDB to securely store patient data, health metrics, and personalized health plans. The app required a database that could comply with healthcare regulations and DynamoDB's security features provided the necessary data protection.

## 7. Travel Booking Website

A travel booking website used DynamoDB to manage hotel listings, customer bookings, and payment transactions. DynamoDB's global tables feature enabled the website to provide low-latency data access to users around the world.

## 8. Video Streaming Service

A video streaming service used DynamoDB to store user preferences, watch history, and subscription details. The service required a database solution that could support rapid scaling to accommodate a growing library of content and user base.

## 9. Educational Technology Platform

An ed-tech platform used DynamoDB to store student progress, course materials, and interactive lesson data. DynamoDB's reliable performance under varying loads ensured a consistent learning experience for users.

## 10. Financial Services Application

A fintech application used DynamoDB for transaction processing, fraud detection, and user account management. The need for high security and fast data access made DynamoDB a suitable choice for the financial sector.

## 11. Retail Inventory Management

A retail company implemented an inventory management system using DynamoDB to track stock levels, supplier data, and purchase orders. The system benefited from DynamoDB's flexible data model and scalability.

## 12. Sports Analytics Platform

A sports analytics platform utilized DynamoDB to process and store real-time sports data, including player statistics and match outcomes. The platform required a database that could handle high-throughput writes during live sporting events.

These case studies demonstrate the versatility and effectiveness of Amazon DynamoDB in supporting various types of applications. From handling large-scale e-commerce transactions to streaming media content and managing IoT device data, DynamoDB has proven to be a robust and scalable solution for modern mobile and web applications.

# Chapter 19: Advanced Data Processing Techniques

## Section 19.1: Stream Processing with DynamoDB Streams

Stream processing is an essential aspect of dealing with real-time data, especially in applications that require immediate responsiveness or analytics. Amazon DynamoDB Streams provides a powerful way to capture and respond to data changes in your DynamoDB tables in real-time. In this section, we explore how to utilize DynamoDB Streams for stream processing, integrating with various AWS services and implementing effective strategies for real-time data handling.

### 1. Introduction to DynamoDB Streams

DynamoDB Streams captures a time-ordered sequence of item-level modifications in any DynamoDB table and stores this information for up to 24 hours. Applications can access this stream and process these changes in real time. This feature is particularly useful for triggering workflows, synchronizing data, or even for replicating changes to other data stores.

### 2. Enabling DynamoDB Streams

To use DynamoDB Streams, you first need to enable it on your DynamoDB table. You can do this using the AWS Management Console, AWS CLI, or the AWS SDKs. When enabling Streams, you can choose the type of information to be stored in the stream, such as keys only, new image, old image, or both.

## 3. Stream Record Structure

Each stream record contains information about a single data modification in the table. This includes the keys of the modified item, the nature of the modification (insert, update, delete), and the before and after images of the item.

## 4. Reading Data from Streams

You can access the data in a DynamoDB Stream directly using the AWS SDK. The SDK allows you to poll the stream and retrieve the stream records. However, a more efficient and scalable approach is to use AWS Lambda, where a Lambda function is triggered for each batch of records from the stream.

## 5. Integration with AWS Lambda

AWS Lambda integration is one of the most powerful features of DynamoDB Streams. By creating a Lambda function and linking it to a DynamoDB Stream, you can process changes in real time. This setup is ideal for a variety of use cases, including real-time analytics, alerts, replication, and more.

## 6. Example Lambda Function for Stream Processing

Here's an example of a simple AWS Lambda function in Python that processes records from a DynamoDB Stream:

```
import boto3

import json

def lambda_handler(event, context):

for record in event['Records']:
```

```
# Process each record
print("Stream record: ", json.dumps(record, indent=2))
return 'Successfully processed records.'
```

## 7. Ordering and Sharding

DynamoDB Streams ensures the order of records within each shard of the stream. However, there may be multiple shards, and records are not ordered across shards. Keep this in mind when designing your stream processing logic.

## 8. Handling Stream Data Volume

The volume of data in a DynamoDB Stream can be significant, especially for tables with high write throughput. Ensure your processing logic and downstream services are capable of handling this volume.

## 9. Security and Access Control

Manage access to DynamoDB Streams using AWS Identity and Access Management (IAM). Ensure that only authorized entities have the necessary permissions to read from and write to the stream.

## 10. Error Handling and Retries

Implement robust error handling in your stream processing logic. AWS Lambda provides automatic retry mechanisms, but you should also handle exceptions and faulty records appropriately to prevent data loss or duplicates.

## 11. Stream Processing Patterns

Consider various stream processing patterns such as filtering, aggregation, transformation, or joining with other data sources. Each pattern suits different use cases and requirements.

## 12. Monitoring and Logging

Monitor your stream processing using Amazon CloudWatch. Keep track of metrics like execution duration, error rates, and throughput. Implement logging within your AWS Lambda function for diagnostic purposes.

## 13. Real-Time Analytics

DynamoDB Streams can be a source for real-time analytics solutions. Integrate with services like Amazon Kinesis Analytics to analyze data on the fly and gain insights from your streaming data.

## 14. Cross-Region Replication

You can use DynamoDB Streams to implement cross-region replication. This is useful for creating geo-distributed applications and improving data locality.

## 15. Data Archiving

Streams can also be used to archive data changes to services like Amazon S3. This is particularly useful for audit trails or historical analysis.

### 16. Scaling Considerations

As your application scales, the number of stream records can increase significantly. Plan your AWS Lambda function's capacity and concurrency settings to handle increased loads.

### 17. Best Practices

Follow best practices for stream processing, such as keeping the processing code idempotent, minimizing the processing time of each record, and efficiently managing resources.

By leveraging DynamoDB Streams for stream processing, you can build applications that respond quickly to data changes, enabling real-time data processing and analytics, and creating reactive, dynamic user experiences.

---

## Section 19.2: Integrating with Data Warehouses

Integrating Amazon DynamoDB with data warehouses can significantly enhance the analytical capabilities of your applications. Data warehouses allow for the storage and analysis of large volumes of data, which is particularly useful for complex queries, reporting, and business intelligence. This section discusses how to integrate DynamoDB with data warehouses like Amazon Redshift and outlines best practices for doing so.

### 1. Understanding the Need for Integration

While DynamoDB excels at handling high-throughput, low-latency operations, it is not optimized for complex analytical queries. Integrating DynamoDB with a data warehouse allows you to perform intensive data analysis that would otherwise be challenging directly on DynamoDB.

## 2. Exporting Data from DynamoDB

The first step in integration is exporting data from DynamoDB. You can use AWS Data Pipeline or create a custom solution to export data to Amazon S3. From S3, data can then be loaded into a data warehouse.

## 3. Using AWS Glue for Data Export

AWS Glue is a fully managed ETL (extract, transform, load) service that makes it easy to prepare and load data for analytics. You can use AWS Glue to transfer data from DynamoDB to Amazon S3 and then into a data warehouse.

## 4. Schema Conversion

When moving data from DynamoDB to a data warehouse, schema conversion is often necessary. DynamoDB's schema-less nature means you will need to define a schema that matches the structure of your data for the data warehouse.

## 5. Incremental Data Load

For efficient data transfer, especially with large datasets, consider incremental data loading. This involves only transferring new or changed data at regular intervals.

## 6. Direct Integration with Amazon Redshift

Amazon Redshift can directly query and load data from Amazon S3. Once your DynamoDB data is exported to S3, you can use Redshift's COPY command to import it into your Redshift data warehouse.

## 7. Data Transformation

Data transformation might be required to optimize the data structure for analytical queries. This can be done using AWS Glue or other data transformation tools.

## 8. Real-time Data Integration

For real-time data integration scenarios, consider using DynamoDB Streams with AWS Lambda to capture changes in DynamoDB and update the data warehouse in near real-time.

## 9. Querying Data

Once your data is in a data warehouse, you can use SQL queries to perform complex analysis, generate reports, and derive insights. Data visualization tools can also be connected to your data warehouse for enhanced reporting.

## 10. Performance Considerations

Optimize the performance of your data warehouse by appropriately structuring your data, indexing, and choosing the right distribution style for your tables in Amazon Redshift.

## 11. Security and Compliance

Ensure that the data transfer and storage in your data warehouse comply with security and privacy standards. Implement encryption, access control, and auditing.

## 12. Cost Management

Monitor and manage the costs associated with data transfer and storage in your data warehouse. Optimize data transfer frequencies and storage utilization to control costs.

## 13. Automated ETL Pipelines

Create automated ETL pipelines for regular data transfers. This reduces manual effort and ensures that your data warehouse has the latest data for analysis.

## 14. Data Warehousing Best Practices

Follow best practices for data warehousing, including data normalization, proper use of star and snowflake schemas, and efficient query design.

## 15. Backup and Recovery

Plan for backup and recovery of your data in the data warehouse. Regular backups ensure that you can recover your data in case of any loss or corruption.

## 16. Monitoring and Logging

Implement monitoring and logging for your ETL processes and data warehouse operations. This helps in tracking performance and troubleshooting issues.

## 17. Scalability

Plan for scalability in your data warehouse solution. As your data grows, your data warehouse should scale to accommodate the increased data volume and query load.

By effectively integrating DynamoDB with a data warehouse, you can significantly enhance your application's ability to perform complex analytics, thereby gaining deeper insights into your data and supporting data-driven decision-making.

## Section 19.3: Machine Learning Applications

Leveraging Amazon DynamoDB in machine learning applications can unlock a myriad of possibilities for data analysis, prediction, and automation. This section will explore how DynamoDB can be integrated with machine learning workflows, tools, and techniques to enhance the capabilities of applications.

### 1. Data Collection and Storage

DynamoDB serves as an efficient platform for collecting and storing data for machine learning. Its ability to handle large volumes of data at high speed makes it ideal for scenarios where data is continuously generated, such as user interactions, IoT sensor data, or real-time event logging.

### 2. Preparing Data for Machine Learning

Before using DynamoDB data in machine learning models, it often needs to be preprocessed. This includes tasks like normalization, handling missing values, encoding categorical variables, and feature selection. AWS Lambda can be used to preprocess data directly from DynamoDB streams.

### 3. Integration with Amazon S3

For machine learning, large datasets are often moved from DynamoDB to Amazon S3, a more cost-effective storage solution for large-scale data. From S3, data can be easily accessed by various machine learning tools and platforms provided by AWS.

## 4. Using AWS Glue for ETL

AWS Glue can automate the extract, transform, and load (ETL) process of data from DynamoDB to Amazon S3. It can prepare and transform the data into a format suitable for machine learning models.

## 5. Machine Learning with Amazon SageMaker

Amazon SageMaker provides a complete environment to build, train, and deploy machine learning models. Data stored in DynamoDB can be exported and utilized in SageMaker for training models using algorithms provided by AWS or your custom algorithms.

## 6. Real-time Predictions

For applications requiring real-time predictions, you can set up an AWS Lambda function to invoke a machine learning model hosted on Amazon SageMaker. The Lambda function can process data from DynamoDB and send it to the model for real-time inference.

## 7. Batch Processing with AWS Batch

For batch processing of machine learning jobs, AWS Batch can schedule and run these jobs using data exported from DynamoDB. This is useful for scenarios where models need to be retrained periodically with new data.

## 8. Machine Learning Model Monitoring

Once a machine learning model is deployed, it's important to continuously monitor its performance. AWS CloudWatch can be used to monitor the model's performance metrics and log any anomalies or errors.

## 9. Feedback Loop for Model Improvement

Implement a feedback loop where the predictions and results from the machine learning model are written back to DynamoDB. This data can then be analyzed to further refine and improve the model.

## 10. Using DynamoDB as a Feature Store

DynamoDB can act as a feature store for your machine learning models. It can store and retrieve feature data used by models for training and inference, benefiting from its low latency and scalability.

## 11. Data Versioning

In machine learning, it's crucial to track different versions of datasets. DynamoDB can maintain different versions of your data, which is vital for replicating model results and auditing.

## 12. Handling Unstructured Data

For unstructured data like images or text, consider storing metadata or references in DynamoDB while keeping the actual data in Amazon S3. This approach leverages DynamoDB's strengths in managing structured data and S3's capabilities for storing large files.

## 13. Security and Compliance

Ensure that your machine learning applications comply with data privacy and security regulations. Use IAM roles and policies to control access to data in DynamoDB and encrypt sensitive data both in transit and at rest.

## 14. Scalable Architecture

Design your architecture to scale both the data storage layer in DynamoDB and the machine learning components. Utilize AWS services that can dynamically scale according to the workload demands.

## 15. Cost Optimization

Be mindful of the costs associated with data storage, processing, and machine learning operations. Regularly monitor and optimize your AWS resource usage to control costs.

## 16. Utilizing AWS Marketplace for Algorithms

Explore the AWS Marketplace for machine learning algorithms that can be directly applied to your data in DynamoDB. This can significantly speed up the development of machine learning applications.

## 17. Custom Machine Learning Models

For specific needs, develop custom machine learning models. You can leverage various machine learning frameworks and languages, such as TensorFlow or Python, and train these models using the data stored in DynamoDB.

By integrating DynamoDB with machine learning workflows and AWS services, you can enhance your applications with predictive analytics, automated decision-making, and advanced data insights, all while leveraging the scalability and performance of DynamoDB.

## Section 19.4: Complex Event Processing (CEP)

Complex Event Processing (CEP) is an advanced technique used to process and analyze streams of data to identify meaningful patterns, trends, and relationships. When integrated with Amazon DynamoDB, CEP can enhance the capabilities of applications to process and react to real-time data effectively. This section explores the integration of DynamoDB with CEP systems, strategies, and best practices.

### 1. Overview of CEP with DynamoDB

CEP involves analyzing data from various sources to detect complex patterns. DynamoDB, with its capacity to handle high-throughput data and integration with AWS Lambda and DynamoDB Streams, serves as an excellent backend for CEP systems.

### 2. Setting Up CEP with DynamoDB Streams

DynamoDB Streams can be utilized to capture data modifications in real-time. These streams can then be fed into CEP engines to analyze patterns as they emerge.

### 3. Real-Time Analytics

Leverage CEP to perform real-time analytics on data changes. This can involve detecting trends, anomalies, or specific event patterns that are significant for business operations or user interactions.

## 4. Integration with AWS Kinesis

Amazon Kinesis is an ideal platform for CEP when working with DynamoDB. Kinesis can consume data from DynamoDB Streams and perform real-time data processing and analytics.

## 5. CEP Engine Selection

Choose a CEP engine that best fits your requirements. AWS offers its own solutions like Amazon Kinesis Analytics, or you can opt for third-party CEP engines that can integrate with AWS services.

## 6. Event Pattern Detection

Design event patterns that are relevant to your application's needs. This can range from simple threshold-based alerts to complex correlations across multiple data streams.

## 7. AWS Lambda for Event Actions

Use AWS Lambda to execute actions based on CEP results. For instance, triggering notifications, updating other systems, or initiating workflows in response to detected event patterns.

## 8. Scalability and Performance

Ensure that your CEP solution scales with the volume of data from DynamoDB. Consider the throughput of DynamoDB Streams and the processing capacity of your CEP engine.

## 9. Data Transformation

Apply necessary data transformations before processing the streams. This can include format changes, enriching data, or filtering irrelevant information.

## 10. Combining Batch and Real-Time Processing

Some scenarios may require a combination of batch and real-time processing. Design your system to handle real-time stream processing while also supporting periodic batch analytics.

## 11. Monitoring CEP Systems

Monitor the performance and output of your CEP system. Use Amazon CloudWatch to keep track of operational metrics and set up alerts for anomalies in the CEP process.

## 12. Security and Compliance

Maintain high security and compliance standards. Ensure data in transit and at rest is encrypted and access is controlled through IAM policies.

## 13. Error Handling

Implement robust error handling in your CEP system. This includes managing incomplete data, stream interruptions, and processing errors.

## 14. Data Retention Policies

Define data retention policies in DynamoDB and your CEP system. Consider how long data should be kept for real-time processing and historical analysis.

## 15. Cost Management

Be mindful of the costs associated with DynamoDB operations, data transfer, and CEP engine usage. Regularly review and optimize resource usage to manage expenses.

### 16. Testing and Simulation

Thoroughly test your CEP system with simulations and real-world data scenarios. This helps in validating pattern detection logic and the overall responsiveness of the system.

### 17. Documentation and Best Practices

Document the architecture, data flow, and processing logic of your CEP system. Adhere to best practices in stream processing and event pattern design.

By incorporating CEP with DynamoDB, you can build sophisticated systems capable of processing and analyzing data streams in real-time, enabling faster decision-making and responsive application behavior.

---

## Section 19.5: Real-Time Analytics and Dashboards

Real-time analytics and dashboards play a crucial role in modern data-driven applications. They provide immediate insights into data changes and trends, allowing organizations to make informed decisions promptly. In this section, we'll explore how Amazon DynamoDB can be integrated with real-time analytics and dashboarding solutions to create dynamic and responsive data visualization tools.

### 1. Leveraging DynamoDB Streams

DynamoDB Streams is a key component for real-time analytics with DynamoDB. It captures changes to data in real time and makes these changes available for processing. To integrate real-time analytics, configure your DynamoDB table to enable streams.

## 2. Choosing a Real-Time Analytics Solution

Select a real-time analytics solution that fits your needs. AWS offers Amazon Kinesis Data Analytics for real-time data processing, which can consume data from DynamoDB Streams. Alternatively, you can explore third-party analytics tools that integrate seamlessly with DynamoDB.

## 3. Data Transformation and Enrichment

Before visualization, you may need to transform and enrich the data from DynamoDB Streams. This can include aggregating data, joining it with other datasets, or applying business-specific logic to prepare it for analysis.

## 4. Building Real-Time Dashboards

Once you have processed and enriched the data, you can start building real-time dashboards. Popular dashboarding tools like Amazon QuickSight, Tableau, or Grafana can connect to your real-time data source and create interactive visualizations.

## 5. Data Visualization Best Practices

Follow best practices for data visualization to ensure your dashboards are informative and easy to interpret. Use appropriate charts, graphs, and widgets to represent the data effectively.

## 6. Real-Time Data Updates

Configure your dashboards to update in real time as new data arrives from DynamoDB Streams. Users should see changes reflected immediately without needing to refresh the page.

## 7. Alerts and Notifications

Implement alerts and notifications within your dashboarding solution. Set up thresholds and triggers to alert users when specific events or anomalies occur in the data.

## 8. User Access Control

Control user access to the real-time dashboards by integrating with AWS Identity and Access Management (IAM). Ensure that only authorized individuals can view and interact with sensitive data.

## 9. Scaling for Performance

As your data volume grows, consider scaling your real-time analytics and dashboarding solutions to handle increased traffic and data processing demands. AWS services like Amazon QuickSight can automatically scale.

## 10. Cost Optimization

Monitor and optimize costs associated with your real-time analytics and dashboards. Some services charge based on usage, so regularly review your usage patterns and adjust resources accordingly.

## 11. Error Handling and Logging

Implement error handling mechanisms in your real-time analytics pipeline. Log errors and exceptions for troubleshooting and debugging purposes.

## 12. Data Retention Policies

Define data retention policies for your real-time analytics. Determine how long historical data should be retained and what data can be purged to manage storage costs.

## 13. Integration with Applications

Integrate your real-time dashboards with your applications. Embed dashboards into web applications or share them with stakeholders through secure access links.

## 14. Performance Monitoring

Monitor the performance of your real-time analytics and dashboards using Amazon CloudWatch or other monitoring tools. Set up alarms to be notified of any performance issues.

## 15. Documentation and Training

Document the architecture and setup of your real-time analytics and dashboards. Provide training to users and administrators to ensure effective utilization of these tools.

## 16. Continuous Improvement

Regularly review and improve your real-time analytics and dashboarding solutions. Adapt to changing data patterns and business requirements to maintain their relevance and effectiveness.

By integrating DynamoDB with real-time analytics and dashboards, you empower your organization with the ability to make informed decisions based on up-to-the-minute data insights. These dynamic visualization tools are instrumental in responding to changing business conditions and ensuring data-driven decision-making.

# Chapter 20: Concluding Perspectives on DynamoDB

In this final chapter, we'll summarize key takeaways and reflect on the journey through Amazon DynamoDB. We'll explore its place in the evolving landscape of database technologies, its role within the broader AWS ecosystem, and offer some parting thoughts on embracing DynamoDB for future projects. Additionally, we'll provide resources and further learning paths for those interested in diving deeper into DynamoDB or related topics.

## Section 20.1: Key Takeaways and Best Practices Recap

Let's start by revisiting the essential lessons and best practices covered throughout this book:

1. **Understanding NoSQL and DynamoDB**: DynamoDB is a NoSQL database that offers high availability, scalability, and low latency. Understand its data model, key-value structure, and the importance of schema flexibility.
2. **Setting Up with Amazon DynamoDB**: Learn how to create an AWS account, navigate the AWS Management Console, set up DynamoDB, and manage security and access.
3. **DynamoDB Core Concepts**: Explore tables, items, attributes, primary keys, and the significance of read and write capacity units. Understand the different types of indexes and data types.
4. **Data Modeling in DynamoDB**: Design efficient tables, handle relationships, and decide between data normalization and denormalization based on your use case.

5. **CRUD Operations in DynamoDB**: Master create, read, update, and delete operations in DynamoDB, including conditional operations and atomic counters.
6. **Advanced Querying Techniques**: Optimize queries and scans, utilize secondary indexes, filter and sort results, and implement pagination and expressions.
7. **Integrating with Application Code**: Explore DynamoDB SDKs for popular programming languages, set up the development environment, and practice basic CRUD operations in code.
8. **Performance Optimization**: Manage throughput, choose between on-demand and provisioned capacity modes, monitor performance with CloudWatch, and leverage caching strategies with DAX.
9. **Scalability and Reliability**: Understand DynamoDB's distributed architecture, use auto scaling, handle spikes, and implement backup and restore strategies for high availability.
10. **Security in DynamoDB**: Control access with IAM roles, implement data encryption at rest and in transit, audit with AWS CloudTrail, and follow data protection best practices.
11. **Advanced Features and Services**: Explore DynamoDB Streams for real-time processing, integrate with Lambda for serverless architectures, manage data export and import, work with Global Tables, and use Time to Live (TTL) for data expiry.
12. **Troubleshooting and Maintenance**: Identify common issues, implement effective logging and monitoring strategies, perform performance tuning, conduct regular maintenance, and plan data upgrades and migrations.
13. **Best Practices in DynamoDB Usage**: Learn design

patterns, ensure data consistency and concurrency control, follow cost-effective strategies, plan for scalability and growth, and optimize data retrieval.

14. **Case Studies and Real-World Applications**: Explore real-world use cases, including e-commerce platforms, IoT solutions, scalable mobile backends, data analytics, and large-scale deployments.
15. **The Future of DynamoDB and NoSQL Databases**: Delve into emerging trends in NoSQL technology, DynamoDB's roadmap, the role of AI and machine learning, its place in big data, and preparing for future challenges and opportunities.

These key takeaways and best practices serve as a foundation for successfully working with DynamoDB. As you embark on your DynamoDB journey, remember that continuous learning and adaptation are essential.

In the following sections, we'll delve into DynamoDB's position within the AWS ecosystem, consider its role in the broader database landscape, and discuss how it can shape the future of data management.

---

## Section 20.2: DynamoDB's Roadmap and Future Features

Amazon DynamoDB has a rich history of evolution and continuous improvement. AWS frequently releases updates and enhancements to meet the growing needs of developers and businesses. In this section, we'll discuss DynamoDB's roadmap and explore some of the anticipated future features and improvements.

### 1. Enhanced Global Tables: DynamoDB Global

Tables provide multi-region, highly available solutions. In the future, we can expect enhancements to make global tables even more versatile and easier to manage. This might include simplified setup and configuration, improved conflict resolution mechanisms, and better latency optimizations.

2. Advanced Consistency Models: While DynamoDB offers strong eventual consistency and transactional support, future updates may introduce more advanced consistency models to cater to specific use cases. This could include options for tunable consistency, allowing developers to choose between strong and eventual consistency on a per-operation basis.

3. Advanced Query and Analytics: DynamoDB's query capabilities are already powerful, but AWS might further enhance its querying and analytical capabilities. Expect improvements in query performance, support for more complex analytical queries, and deeper integration with AWS analytics services.

4. Enhanced Security Features: Security is a top priority for AWS, and DynamoDB is no exception. We can anticipate the addition of more fine-grained access control options, enhanced encryption features, and improved auditing and monitoring capabilities.

5. Integration with AI and ML Services: As AI and machine learning become integral to various applications, DynamoDB is likely to offer tighter integration with AWS AI/ML services. This could simplify the process of using machine learning

models for tasks such as predictive analytics and recommendation systems.

6. Serverless Architectures: DynamoDB is already a popular choice for serverless applications. In the future, AWS might provide even more seamless integration with AWS Lambda and other serverless computing services, making it easier to build event-driven applications.

7. Data Lake Integration: With the growing popularity of data lakes for storing and analyzing massive datasets, DynamoDB might offer improved integration with AWS data lake services like Amazon S3 and AWS Glue. This would facilitate easier data movement and analytics.

8. Performance Optimization: AWS continuously works on improving performance. Expect future updates to include optimizations for specific workloads and use cases, ensuring DynamoDB remains a high-performance database service.

9. Developer Tooling: AWS is likely to invest in improving developer tooling around DynamoDB. This could involve enhancements to the AWS SDKs, improved debugging and monitoring tools, and better local development environments.

10. Cost Optimization: While DynamoDB offers cost-effective scaling options, AWS may introduce further cost optimization features, helping businesses save on their DynamoDB expenses without compromising performance.

It's important to note that AWS's development roadmap is influenced by customer feedback and emerging industry trends. As a DynamoDB user, you can actively contribute to the service's direction by providing feedback and participating in AWS forums and user groups. DynamoDB's future looks promising, and staying updated with its latest features and capabilities will be essential for developers and businesses.

---

## Section 20.3: The Role of AI and Machine Learning

The role of AI (Artificial Intelligence) and ML (Machine Learning) in the future of Amazon DynamoDB and NoSQL databases, in general, is poised to be transformative. As businesses increasingly leverage AI and ML technologies to gain insights, optimize operations, and deliver personalized experiences, databases like DynamoDB are evolving to meet these demands. In this section, we will explore how AI and ML are expected to play a significant role in DynamoDB's future.

**1. Predictive Analytics: One of the key applications of AI and ML is predictive analytics. DynamoDB can benefit from predictive modeling to forecast future data trends and help businesses make proactive decisions. For example, an e-commerce platform using DynamoDB can employ ML algorithms to predict customer preferences and optimize product recommendations in real-time.**

**2. Recommendation Engines: AI-powered recommendation engines are crucial for platforms like streaming services, e-commerce, and content websites. DynamoDB can integrate with ML models**

to provide personalized recommendations based on user behavior and preferences. This enhances user engagement and drives revenue growth.

3. Data Quality and Anomaly Detection: ML algorithms can be employed to detect data anomalies and ensure data quality in DynamoDB. This is especially important for industries like finance, healthcare, and manufacturing, where data accuracy is critical for decision-making and compliance.

4. Natural Language Processing (NLP): DynamoDB can leverage NLP models to extract insights from unstructured text data stored within the database. This enables sentiment analysis, chatbots, and content recommendation systems to provide more intelligent and context-aware responses.

5. Real-time Insights: By integrating DynamoDB with ML services like Amazon SageMaker, businesses can gain real-time insights from their data. ML models can process streaming data from DynamoDB Streams to identify patterns, detect anomalies, and trigger automated actions.

6. Auto-Scaling with AI: AI-driven auto-scaling can optimize DynamoDB's resource allocation. ML algorithms can predict traffic patterns and adjust read/write capacity automatically, ensuring optimal performance while minimizing costs.

7. Data Classification and Tagging: ML models can classify and tag data within DynamoDB based on content, sensitivity, or relevance. This aids in data governance, compliance, and access control, making

**it easier to manage and secure sensitive data.**

**8. Personalized User Experiences: DynamoDB can store user profiles and behavioral data, allowing businesses to create highly personalized user experiences. ML models can analyze this data to tailor content, offers, and interactions in real-time.**

**9. Operational Efficiency: AI-driven automation can improve operational efficiency in database management. Tasks like database optimization, indexing, and backup scheduling can be automated, reducing the administrative burden on IT teams.**

**10. Integration with AI Services: AWS offers a wide range of AI and ML services that can seamlessly integrate with DynamoDB. These include services for training custom ML models, natural language understanding, image recognition, and more.**

In conclusion, the integration of AI and ML technologies into Amazon DynamoDB is set to empower businesses to extract more value from their data, enhance customer experiences, and streamline operations. Developers and data engineers should stay informed about these advancements to leverage DynamoDB effectively for AI and ML-driven applications. As AI and ML continue to evolve, DynamoDB will remain a powerful and flexible database service that can adapt to the changing needs of modern applications.

---

## Section 20.4: DynamoDB in the Context of Big Data

Amazon DynamoDB, as a NoSQL database service, plays a crucial role in the context of big data. In this section, we will explore how

DynamoDB fits into the landscape of big data technologies and its significance in handling large volumes of data efficiently.

**1. Scalability and Performance: DynamoDB's ability to scale horizontally makes it well-suited for big data workloads. It can handle massive amounts of data and provide low-latency responses, ensuring that applications can seamlessly scale to accommodate high data ingestion rates.**

**2. Data Ingestion: DynamoDB can serve as a landing zone for real-time data ingestion from various sources, such as IoT devices, web applications, and logs. Its fast write capabilities make it suitable for handling streaming data, which is a common requirement in big data processing.**

**3. Data Storage: While DynamoDB excels in real-time data access, it can also serve as a persistent data store for historical data in big data architectures. By integrating with data lakes and data warehouses, DynamoDB can be part of a comprehensive data storage strategy.**

**4. Integration with Analytics Services: DynamoDB seamlessly integrates with AWS analytics services like Amazon Redshift, Amazon Athena, and Amazon QuickSight. This allows businesses to run complex queries, analyze historical data, and generate insights from DynamoDB data.**

**5. Time-Series Data: Many big data use cases involve time-series data, such as sensor readings, logs, and financial market data. DynamoDB's support for TTL (Time to Live) and efficient range queries makes it**

suitable for storing and querying time-series data.

6. Real-Time Analytics: DynamoDB Streams enables real-time analytics by capturing and processing changes to data in near-real-time. This feature is valuable for applications that require real-time insights and actions based on data updates.

7. Serverless Processing: AWS Lambda, a serverless compute service, can be integrated with DynamoDB to perform data processing and transformation tasks. This serverless approach is cost-effective and scalable, making it ideal for big data workloads.

8. Machine Learning Integration: DynamoDB can store data that is used for training machine learning models. By integrating with AWS SageMaker or other ML services, businesses can leverage DynamoDB data to build predictive models and make data-driven decisions.

9. Data Governance: DynamoDB's security and access control features are crucial for maintaining data governance in big data scenarios. Fine-grained IAM (Identity and Access Management) permissions ensure that only authorized users can access sensitive data.

10. Cost Optimization: DynamoDB offers flexible pricing options, including on-demand and provisioned capacity modes. This flexibility allows organizations to optimize costs based on the specific requirements of their big data workloads.

In summary, Amazon DynamoDB is an integral component of modern big data architectures. Its ability to handle high volumes of data, low-latency access, and seamless integration with other AWS services positions it as a key player in the big data ecosystem. As organizations continue to deal with growing data volumes, DynamoDB will play a central role in helping them derive insights and value from their data assets. Developers and data engineers should consider DynamoDB's capabilities when designing and implementing big data solutions on AWS.

---

## Section 20.5: Preparing for Future Challenges and Opportunities

As the field of data management and technology continues to evolve, it is essential for organizations to prepare for future challenges and seize new opportunities. In this final section, we will discuss strategies and considerations to ensure that your DynamoDB-powered applications remain agile and adaptable in a rapidly changing landscape.

**1. Stay Informed: Keep abreast of the latest developments in DynamoDB and the broader AWS ecosystem. AWS regularly introduces new features and services, so staying informed is crucial to leverage advancements effectively.**

**2. Architect for Flexibility: Design your DynamoDB tables and data models with flexibility in mind. Anticipate potential changes in data requirements and usage patterns. Use adaptive schema design principles to accommodate evolving needs.**

**3. Continuous Optimization: Regularly review and**

optimize your DynamoDB tables for cost and performance. Utilize tools like AWS Trusted Advisor and Amazon CloudWatch to monitor usage and identify areas for improvement.

4. Security and Compliance: Stay vigilant about security and compliance requirements. DynamoDB provides encryption, access controls, and auditing features to help meet regulatory standards. Regularly audit and update your security policies.

5. Scaling Strategy: As your application scales, revisit your scaling strategy. Evaluate whether to switch between on-demand and provisioned capacity modes based on cost and performance considerations.

6. Disaster Recovery: Ensure that you have robust disaster recovery plans in place. DynamoDB's backup and restore capabilities can be essential in recovering data in case of unexpected outages or data loss.

7. Machine Learning Integration: Explore opportunities to integrate machine learning into your DynamoDB-powered applications. ML can uncover insights from data and automate decision-making processes.

8. Multi-Region Deployment: Consider deploying DynamoDB tables across multiple AWS regions to enhance fault tolerance and reduce latency for global users. Implement global tables for seamless data replication.

9. Monitoring and Alerting: Implement comprehensive monitoring and alerting solutions to

detect and respond to issues proactively. AWS CloudWatch and AWS Lambda can automate remediation tasks.

10. Cost Management: Continuously optimize your DynamoDB costs. Leverage cost analysis tools and regularly review your capacity provisioning to avoid overprovisioning.

11. Training and Skill Development: Invest in training and skill development for your team. AWS offers certifications and training courses that can enhance your team's expertise in DynamoDB and related technologies.

12. Community Engagement: Engage with the DynamoDB and AWS community. Participate in forums, attend conferences, and join user groups to learn from others' experiences and share your knowledge.

13. Experiment and Innovate: Encourage a culture of experimentation and innovation. DynamoDB's flexible schema and serverless capabilities make it an ideal platform for prototyping and exploring new ideas.

14. Documentation and Documentation: Maintain detailed documentation of your DynamoDB tables, schemas, and application architecture. This documentation is invaluable for onboarding new team members and troubleshooting.

15. Feedback Loop: Establish a feedback loop with AWS support and your AWS account team. Provide

**feedback on your experiences with DynamoDB and share insights on potential improvements.**

By embracing these strategies and remaining adaptable, organizations can position themselves to thrive in a dynamic technological landscape. DynamoDB's scalability, reliability, and integration capabilities make it a powerful asset in addressing future challenges and seizing emerging opportunities. Whether you are running mission-critical applications or exploring innovative use cases, DynamoDB can be a cornerstone of your data strategy for years to come.

www.ingramcontent.com/pod-product-compliance
Lightning Source LLC
LaVergne TN
LVHW090301210926
848480LV00001B/96
* 9 7 9 8 2 2 4 2 7 5 6 2 5 *